JAILBREAK

The Beginning

Rune Larsen

JAILBREAK
The Beginning

Published by Author - Rune Larsen

www.SecretRevelations.com

ISBN; 978-82-93411-00-0

Cover design by Panagiotis Lampridis

"Thanks be to God, who gives us the victory through our Lord Jesus Christ."

(1 Corinthians 15:57)

Preface

The day I met Jesus in the Vigeland Park in Oslo on a day in May 2007.
A radical meeting with the Lord Himself made my life immediately completely changed. I was born again.
-From this day, my spiritual battle began against Satan and the demons in the spiritual sphere.

Eventually became a 'church' in Oslo, a place for my family and me. What I thought was the Assembly of God, a fellowship that loved God with all their heart, a fellowship that would follow the Lord and His commandments.
-It turned out not be the true church they claimed to be.

One day in life, something happened to me that I had not expected. I had to take a stand against what everyone told me was the real, the pure, the growing healthy congregation.
Should I continue to be like them, or should I break out of the control and get into what the Lord had for me?
-The choice was easy. I choose the Lord.

Most of the believers I have met over the years have only one question for you when you meet them for the first time; 'Which church are you in, or what church do you come from?'
This question I have been able to answer because I took a settlement with the tradition around what they call churches today, and sought God for the revelation about what a church is.

There is absolutely no doubt; The traditional "church" is a perfect stronghold Satan has managed to accomplish since Jesus left the earth.

If today's "churches" are so free and correct, it is strange that they have the same structure as a Catholic and Lutheran church. It is Sunday that applies, and the priest has not been removed but replaced by a pastor.

The Bible shows us in all simplicity that a pastor is in the ministry of help. But he is almost hailed as the almighty one.
It is an incorrect and a very unhealthy way to run a fellowship.

It's not the pastor or church you're going to follow. It is Jesus Christ; We all must follow.
-You are to show God that you take Him seriously.

If you are someone who follows a church with a pastor as the leader, you will become as they are - one who believes that Christian life is within four walls on a Sunday.
Jesus said, Go! We say, No, I do not have that call.
-This kind of faith and statement is not according to God's will.

I have chosen to call this book JailBreak because what we look at as a congregation is, in most cases, a control organ and not the free church they proclaim to be. That was what I painfully experienced.

It was like a prison, surrounded by people who express their willingness to serve the Lord, but the fruit of their daily routine indicates and shows something completely different.

Titus 1:16 explains in simplicity what I stood above.
"They profess to know God, but in works they deny Him, being abominable, disobedient, and disqualified for every good work."

-Easily explained; They confess their faith but deny it with their actions.

This world is full of sick and lost people. Who is the one who shall go out and preach the gospel to them? Is it the church leaders? The Pastor? The Prophet? The Evangelist? The Apostle? Or the Teacher's task to send out those who will heal and proclaim the gospel of Jesus Christ in the four corners of the world?
-Or is it our responsibility to come into an understanding of this?

It is the Lord who will train you. It is in His presence you will be molded as He wants. It is when you are obedient to His commandments; Your eyes will open up to the truth.

Get into a position with your life wherever possible, and get trained in **all things**. (John 14:26)

Religiosity is something we must be aware of
Satan walks around like a roaring lion, seeking someone to devour. This makes your Christian life much more severe than what we often imagine. Those who think they are matured in Christ are not. You will start to understand this when you take

the written words of the Lord seriously and begin to live a life with and for Him.

All the singing and dancing classes in today's "churches" must be replaced with sincere teachings. True and healthy teaching that deals with sanctification - repentance, and the Lord himself as the only centerpiece. A doctrine that contains what it takes for the lost to be saved.

You are in a war where Satan and the demons are after us all the time. The state of the world today, 2019, is much worse than it was on Sodom's days.
-Sin has almost no limits.

Today;
We live in a time where more than 20000 children die of human-made poverty and ungodliness every single day.

Today;
We use hours upon hours weekly to prepare for "Sunday" dance gala performance in the congregation.

Have you ever thought why there is a need for entertainment in the 'church?' What is the one trying to achieve in what is called God's house, a place where Almighty God should be a focal point. His will, His presence is what should have been the focus. But that's not the way it is.
-What has gone wrong here?

-There is no urge in the hearts of the believers to see the power of God to change this world. We are too comfortable and busy with; I, myself, and I. Most are satisfied with themselves and theirs.

The Lord is not impressed with the congregation when He had to write in His book, "The harvest truly is plentiful, but the laborers are few."

Today;
You only need to enter a credit card number on the screen, and we will have free access to the most depraved pornographic violence and abuse material.

Today;
It is not the unsaved people that are of importance to the churches. We live and breathe within the greenhouse (church) four walls, well gathered with corresponding plants. Religious believers cannot cope with wild plants. They have lived a life in a greenhouse, only with the same type of plants. They become fertilized and watered but have never been shown other plants (humans) outside the greenhouse.
-Religiosity makes it impossible to cope with people in the big world. Ie ordinary people.

If you are going to be the light to those who live in the dark, what do you think must be done now? Should you continue to be one who just hides among other plants inside the greenhouse, or will you become obedient to what the Lord says you shall do?

Today;

It is not many who seek God as we shall seek Him. We are not intervened in becoming a man or woman of God. But laziness shows its origin with a bad conscience; We go to church. That's enough!

-If we had sought God in the right way, there had been millions of believers who had lived a life in the power of the Holy Spirit, out among those who do not have Jesus Christ as Lord.

Ekklesia, the invisible church

When we see how the disciples had fellowship, there is something we must notice. "They came together with the same mind." To agree, that is the case.

-Let me explain in all simplicity; You prove nothing to go in a church on a Sunday. Doing that does not mean you are doing the right thing. Because, if the congregation came together with the same mind, the whole structure would have been different. They all agree that Jesus is Lord, but most of them have different opinions on how and what to do when it becomes the work for the Lord. And if they do not have the same mind here, it is not a congregation of people with the same mind, but a congregation of people who have compromised God's written words.

Should you have the same mind like me, you must agree with the Lord and His commands. It is not enough to agree with me in a prayer meeting or on a Sunday afternoon in 'church.'
Are you willing to do as He says, humble yourself and stop doing all the works of the flesh, seek and love Him with all your power and all your heart, be willing to go out into the world with His gospel? Then you have agreed with the Lord. If you

meet another believer who did the same thing (living in), there will be an invisible agreement between you.

-This is to have the same mind, and this is the Ekklesia. Here we see that it can be difficult to become a "member."

You become nothing until you have agreed with the Lord Himself.

More than ever, it is imperative that God's people engage

-Grab your spiritual weapons and follow Jesus Christ, our Lord, and Savior.

CONTENTS

CHAPTER 1

From death to life

The year was 2007
I had grown up in a home in Norway without God.
-At the age of 37, my whole life fell apart.
Whatever could go wrong in my life had gone wrong, and to top
it all, I was now back living in my old room at my parent's
place.

Many times over the years, I had thought about the meaning of
life, but never really found the right answer. Nor had anybody in
my family found the answer.
-It was a real tragedy.

Watching countless episodes of The Big Bang Theory on Dis-
covery Channel did not give me a satisfactory answer either. I
knew several atheists that denied the existence of a Creator, but
that did not seem to add up in my mind.
-Something was very wrong.

When I was 20 years old, a friend told me one day that he had
become a Christian, and he said that I should 'think' about
things in my life.
I heard what he said but had no idea what he meant.

Garbage

One day I started a job driving a garbage truck in Oslo. The work environment in this company was not the best. The men only talked about alcohol, women, and sport in the lunch and coffee breaks. They told me that the Administrative Director of the company was a Christian, but that he never mixed with the 'boys,' which suited us fine.

There was a small laundry facility in the company where the employees washed their work clothes. We brought in chairs and a coffee machine so that we could meet there before work started, and after the working day was over.
We spent many hours in our little room.

One day a man came into the room. I had seen him many times before but never really talked to him. His name was Roi. As the weeks went by, Roi and I met almost daily in the laundry. It did not take long before I realized that Roi was not like the other men. He never took part in the awful sex and drinking stories exchanged between the men every day.
The other men told me that Roi was religious. I did not pay this much attention, and everyday life continued as usual.

As Roi and I got to know each other better, he started to bring Jesus into the conversation. It was all a bit strange, as every time he said something about Jesus, his face lit up. I did not understand it then, but after later, I realized he was a born again Christian.

Time passed, and we came to know each other better and better. There was no doubt he was enthusiastic about his ministry.

Months went by

As Roi and I had different jobs, we could only meet in the laundry room. However, one day, something happened. The Transport Manager decided we were to work together.

We worked for a municipal company, and the working speed was not the most effective.

On our first day together, Roi started to talk about Jesus, earthquakes, and a whole lot about what the Bible tells us. It was too much for me, so I told him to close his mouth. As soon as I had said it, I thought to myself - why did I say that?
The atmosphere over the next few hours on the job was unpleasant.

The next day Roi started talking about Jesus again, just like the day before, and he didn't stop until the end of our shift. By that time, I was quite exhausted and not because of the work itself. There was no doubt that Satan was trying to stop the whole thing. Although I didn't know any scriptures at that time, Ephesians 6:12 tells us who we are fighting against, and it was not Roi in this case.

The battle begins

Roi and I did not work together again after these two days. However, the next three months were the worst I had ever experienced in all my 37 years. Frustration and racing thoughts bombarded me all the time.

-I did not get a moment's peace from it all.

Just like the verse from Ephesians 6:16, Satan kept shooting his darts at me with temptations at every turn. As the days progressed, I became more and more besides myself. It seemed like I saw an internal film of my life. Later I understood that this was the run-up to repentance from my sinful life.

My thought life began to turn around, and I felt that I had no choice but to follow it. Each day was worse than the other, and I finished work in a state of total exhaustion. It did not tie-up with the kind of work I did.

Every evening I sat in my room reflecting over the day's progress. Each time the Lord spoke to me as only He can, and it was to my inner self. Afterward, it became clear that the Lord himself had been evangelizing me in those three months after Roi, and I stopped working together.

The Lord spoke to me daily in such a way that eventually led me to full repentance.

Google led me to the final decision
One day the voice came again, and I heard the words, "You must become a Christian."

-It felt strange, and I pondered over it for a few days.

Then one day in May 2007 it happened

My head was full of thoughts about becoming a Christian, and the more I thought about it, the worse it became.

-I had no peace.

I also had no idea about how you became a Christian, so in desperation, I turned on my computer, found google.com, and typed the words; **How to become a Christian.**

There were different answers to my question, but eventually, I understood that repentance from my sins and a prayer to Jesus was what I needed to do. I printed out the sinner's prayer and put it in my pocket.

The racing thoughts calmed down, and it seemed as my inner self had already made a decision.

One day after work, I sat on my bed just passing the time, although God had shown me what I needed to do.

-I needed to repent from all sin in my life!

At the park

One day I decided I had to do something about it. The local park was the place I chose to use the note about repentance I had in my pocket.

I was quite nervous about it, but I told my parents that I was going out for a while.

Each step brought me closer to the living God, who now called me into fellowship with Him. I could not believe it - I had not achieved much in my life, but the Lord and Savior Jesus Christ, who was scourged and crucified for my sake, was calling me.

The sinner was now going to repent of all his sin and receive the miracle of salvation.

I chose the local park because I wanted peace around me, and that was not always possible in my room at home. At the rear of the park, was a massive monument called the Monolith, and it was here among all the statues that I decided I would read the sinner's prayer.

The small note

I had checked that it was still there many times during the last few days. Just as I decided to take out the note, a bus full of Japanese tourists turned up to see the Monolith and take pictures. What happens now, I thought? I was just about to make the most important decision in my life, and all these people were here. However, I should get on with it and took the note out of my pocket.

-Immediately, the Japanese tourists disappeared.

I shouted out loud, "God, if you exist, come here now!"
I was shaking all over and had a lump in my throat that almost stopped me from speaking. I carried on, shouting, "Jesus, I repent of all the sins in my life, forgive me for all the wrong I have done. Come and be Lord of my life; I want to become a Christian now.

I was crying and almost screaming when Jesus appeared. Suddenly I felt a weight lifted from my shoulders, and the pressure on my chest and stomach disappeared. I could breathe even though I gasped like a whale. It continued for 10 to 15 minutes.

What a release, what a heavenly experience, and what a living God we serve!

"Dear Heavenly Father, I thank you and praise you for receiving a sinner like me. Thank you that you paid for the sin of the world on the cross at Calvary and gave your life for me. I thank you with all my heart that I have now received the miracle of salvation and become a Christian."
-In Jesus' name, Amen.

Light as a feather
Never in my 37 years had I felt anything like this. I was ex-hausted, yet at the same time, I felt as light as a feather and felt such inner peace; It was undoubtedly from heaven.
The problem was now to stand upright. I was empty and had no strength left, yet there was a sense of great joy in me.
I hung over the fence by the monument to try to regain my breath and strength. I laughed and cried at the same time as I kept on thanking Jesus for the heavenly work He did on Calvary.
-I was now part of that work.

I had now repented from all the sins in my life. I was now a Christian.

The walk home that generally took 20 minutes seemed to last for hours, yet I felt such incredible joy.

That night in my room, I kept going over the events of the day and said to myself, it's done.

Israel

Roi and I left our jobs as garbage truck drivers and never met each other again. One day many years later, a friend of mine, Kjell Gunnar, was on a trip to Israel. He stayed at a hotel where some of the staff were Norwegians. At that particular time, I was in the Philippines preaching the gospel.

One day a text message came in from Kjell Gunnar, telling about the hotel with the Norwegian staff. The personnel often ate their meals together with the guests at the hotel. One of the staff members started to share a testimony about a man he had worked with many years ago and how he was a hard nut to crack. Kjell Gunnar said that he knew that man, his name is Rune. He is in the Philippines preaching the Lord's gospel.

Yes, it was none other than Roi sitting at the table telling the story.
Imagine the jubilation over an old sinner that was now on the other side of the world serving the Lord.

-What a mighty God we serve.

Notes;

_____

_____

_____

CHAPTER 2

Born again

I give Jesus all honor for my salvation. Just by the fact that He would receive a sinner like me, He would do the same for you, no matter who you are or how great your sin is. Jesus will always accept you and forgives even the most grotesque sin. He does this when you decide to repent of your sins, turn to Him, and trust Him as your Lord and Savior.

The Bible tells us: "Come to Me, <u>all</u> you who labor and are heavy laden, and I will give you rest." (Matthew 11:28)

The word **all** comes from the Greek word **pas**. That means; Everyone, all who exist.
What a wonderful promise.

The Bible tells us;
I (Jesus) am the Way, the Truth and the Life. No man comes to the Father except through Me. (John 14:6 - Hebrews 10:19-20)

The Bible
I could not get enough of the written word of God during the first year of my salvation. I read the New Testament 5 times and the Old Testament once.

There was a daily hunger in me to devour the word of God that I cannot describe. The spiritual battle was also a part of my everyday life, as Satan and his hordes hated the new life I had and tried everything to destroy it. I realized there was only one thing to do, and that was to; Draw near to God, and He will draw near to you. (James 4:8)

Reinhard Bonnke

The first time I heard about Reinhard Bonnke and his crusades drew my attention. I surfed the Internet and found lots of information about him on YouTube and his website. Bonnke sometimes has over a million people at his crusades in Africa. I felt that this was something for me.

The simple way that Bonnke preached the Gospel was the essence of what fascinated me. It was down to earth, simple and with the power of the Holy Spirit. None of the ways we sometimes see today with shaking and bodily manifestations that are more demonic manifestations than God.
It is never about getting a 'touch' from God that leads to shaking and jerking but about coming into a deep intimate relationship with Jesus Christ. That is what should be central in any church or congregation. I did try out a few other ministries for a short time but found most of them strange to my belief.

At this stage, I was the only member of my family to receive salvation. It became difficult for me to be around members of the family, as I was not interested in talking about the things of the world anymore - I just wanted more of Jesus.

I realized that I needed a fellowship with other Christians, and found a church in Oslo that eventually became my spiritual home. (I thought)

Baptism

A Sunday, the church was baptizing people, something I had not thought about much as I was still relatively 'new' on the way. However, one day, a hunger came over me to be baptized, and I knew I had to get into the water very soon. I decided to ask some members of the church if I could be baptized. For some reason, it proved to be difficult, but I never found out why.

The hunger in me increased, and I became desperate. I went on to the Internet and found a church announcing baptism the following week. I contacted them and arranged for my wife and me to baptize. The day arrived, and with joy in our hearts, we drove to the place where the baptism would take place. The baptismal pool was part of the stage, so after we stepped up onto the scene, they asked us if we would like to give our testimony first, which we did.

I went into the water first, and after the pastor said a few words, he pushed me backward so that my whole body went under the water. On the way down, I said, "Here I come, Jesus!"
I was only under the water a few seconds, and I knew that all my sins become erased, and I came up again like a new person. Straight afterward, my wife did the same thing.

In the weeks following my baptism, I experienced the same heavenly presence as I had when I received Jesus as my Savior in the park.

Hebrew and Greek

The Bible has 66 books. The Old Testament is translated from Hebrew and the New Testament from Greek.

Both the English and Norwegian languages give inadequate explanations, while Greek is a vibrant language. One word from Greek can mean up to 25-30 different terms.

If we look at the word baptism, what does it mean?

The Bible tells us in Matthew 3:16 that when Jesus baptized, He came up immediately from the water. Baptized comes from the Greek word "Baptizo," which means; immerse, submerge, full immersion.

Growing in Christ

As time went on, I became a regular at my new church fellowship. They arranged various courses, and I attended all of them. My hunger for the Lord grew, and every day became a new chapter with the Lord. I was ready for everything that the Lord had for me, even though I did not know what it meant at the time.

One thing I understood quite early on was that demons work intensively in Christian circles. Many of the people in leadership positions in a congregation are often very nice people. However, they usually have a hidden agenda to control other persons.

Everything seems to be fine until you begin to suggest to them the following;

1. We should set people free at the prayer meetings.

2. Let us go out and look for people who need healing.

3. All the congregation should be out on the streets preaching the Gospel.

If you start looking for these things in your church, you will soon get opposition from the leadership. If this happens, it shows that you are in a 'church' that wants to control you and your wallet. Our God is not complicated, so it is easy to do His works when you belong to His kingdom. It is just a matter of having faith to do the works He has prepared for us in line with the scriptures.

As time went by, I came to know the people in the church better and joined a cell group for men. We met every Tuesday, and I remember I looked forward to these meetings. At least this was the case in the beginning. I had hoped for a long time that I would make friends with some men that had faith in what the Bible teaches us - namely, to cast out demons and heal the sick. It proved to be very difficult as there was nobody in the group that had such faith.

As I was not yet a member of the church, I dropped the issue and decided to wait until I knew them better.

Baptism in the Holy Spirit

The first time I heard about a heavenly language (speaking in tongues), it aroused my interest. A friend told me about speaking in a language that only God could understand, and it was only through the Holy Spirit, you will have this language. I said to my friend that I wanted to have this language and wondered how I could get it? He told me I needed to be baptized in the Holy Spirit.

I pondered almost every day about this "strange" language, and it took me nearly a year before I was baptized in the Holy Spirit and started to speak in tongues.
One day the church announced they were holding a Victory Weekend. Bible study and deliverance were the topics. I decided to take part in the course.
They gave us study material to go through before the course, and I read it eagerly so I could answer the questions as best I could.

With only four days to go before the course started, I looked forward to it as a small child. We were encouraged to fast the last three days before the course began. It was a real challenge for me only to drink water, but I managed to keep to the fast and arrived on the first day of the course, ready to start.
The first day was intensive, and on the second day, I went to a room with one of the course leaders, where I had to go through all the questions I had answered. We read through the answers, prayed and I repented of everything I needed to. Jesus, my deliverer, did not disappoint me.

On the last evening, they prayed for those of us who wanted to be baptized in the Holy Spirit. During the praise and worship, a woman standing next to me began to shout out in tongues.

The people on either side of me lay on the floor, shrieking and crying in a way I had never seen before.

I thought to myself, Now you must come to me Jesus, I need more of you.

Then it happened. As I stood there with my eyes closed, my lips began to tremble, and suddenly they began to move automatically. I was speaking in tongues.

Although the baptism in the Holy Ghost is not a baptism in tounges, but baptism in power. (Dunamis)
-All Christian need the baptism in the Holy Ghost to become an effective witness to the unsaved.

The baptism in the Holy Ghost was another powerful experience like the others;

1. Salvation in the park - A powerful divine experience.

2. Baptism in water - A powerful divine experience.

3. Baptism in the Holy Spirit - A powerful divine experience.

What a fantastic God we have
At the end of the course, we got awarded with a diploma which I was pleased to receive. There was an offer to become a member of the church, so I decided to join.
-Now the battle was on.

16

Notes;

_____

_____

_____

_____

_____

_____

_____

_____

_____

_____

_____

_____

CHAPTER 3

The new life

The new life became alive. My worldly sunglasses were off, and the Lord began to show me many things through the scriptures. Everywhere I saw things differently than I had previously, while at the same time, I began to react to how people behaved and spoke.

There was no doubt in my mind - I was born again.

I experienced a fantastic time in the first few months, but I felt something was missing. I said to the Lord that I need a wife by my side. She must come from Asia but not Thailand, and she must be a Christian and have a positive outlook on life. She turned up three months later, and after a period of another three months, I proposed to her under the Eiffel Tower in Paris.

The Cell Group

I was now a member of a cell group in the church. Most of the men found it difficult to take part as they felt it was a duty. It was never a duty to me, and I looked forward eagerly to the meetings. Here I met 'brothers' in Christ, talked about life, and read the Word of God. The pastor led the group and decided what the theme would be for the meeting. He downloaded the topic from a website, but I felt it was not the right way to do things. I suggested that each member could ask the Lord what they should share with the group. The pastor did not agree to this suggestion as he was afraid to let others lead the meeting. (Here we see to controlling manipulator in action)

Once we met at the home of the pastor, but the meeting did not go well.
After the Bible study, I suggested we should pray for each other. We stood in a line facing each other to pray, and after we finished with one person, we should move on to the next. The idea was that this way, everyone would receive prayer. We did not end in time for coffee, and I was told it was unnecessary to pray for each other. I thought this was very strange as it is never wrong to pray for other people.

They claim to be Christians, but their actions deny this
"They profess to know God, but in works they deny Him, being abominable, disobedient, and disqualified for every good work." (Titus 1:16)

Nothing but religion from man.
If you are in this kind of group, there is only one thing I would say, that is, the ship is sinking get off. Take a step in faith, trust the Holy Spirit as He will teach you all things. (John 14:26)

Prayer meetings
When you are a new Christian, it is quite normal not to be so active in reaching others outside the church. It is often enough to spend time in the presence of the Lord. Years and years of

strongholds begin to shatter and split. The more time you spend with the Lord, the closer you come to the Lord.

If you are available for Him, He will work intensively on your salvation. He will show you in detail what He wants you to do.

The prayer meetings arranged by the church took place in a small room, even though there was plenty of room in the large building. It was a tradition at these meetings that everyone stood still with closed eyes and bowed heads.

-Nobody opened their eyes until the pastor said the traditional closing prayer.

Once a month, the church arranged an all-night prayer meeting. Many more people attended this meeting than the regular prayer meetings during the week. It was not long before the prayer meetings became uncomfortable for me. The Lord began to show me that many of the people at the prayer meetings were struggling.

One day, in the middle of the prayer meeting, I said to Jesus that I had enough and asked him to show me someone, I could pray for. I opened my eyes and saw a woman dressed in red standing directly opposite me. I walked over to her, put my hands on her shoulder, and asked if I could pray for her. She lifted her head, smiled, and said yes. As I prayed, she began to weep, with tears streaming down her face. It was clear that the Lord was on the move.

I went back to my place as I did not want to upset anyone, and asked the Lord again to show me a person who needed prayer.

I went to pray for a woman standing on my right-hand side, and the same thing happened to her. I thought to myself that there was no doubt the Lord had no objection to us praying for each other. It was just something they did not do in the church. -All doctrine must come from the Word of God, not through human tradition. (Colossians 2:8)

Forbidden to pray for other people during prayer meetings
I continued to pray for the people at the prayer meeting, and it resulted in something special happening each time. Several times when I laid hands on people, they immediately fell to the floor.

The Bible mentions casting out demons a lot, and all Christians need to know the biblical meaning of this and how to do it. We ought to obey the Word of God, not traditional leadership in a church. If you are not available to other people, you will not see a single demon.

People become worn out because demons have a hold on their lives. If you believe and act on the Word of God, then the demons must flee. Ephesians 6:12 tells us who our enemy is and that he is trying to destroy us. The vital issue in Ephesians 6 is not who we are fighting but how to stand against them.

As the days and months progressed, I grew in the Lord more and more. If we are willing and available, the Lord will use us, just like He did in the prayer meetings. I made myself available to God, and He met people through my faith in Him. After a while,

the leadership in the church came with a new rule. It is forbidden to pray for people during prayer meetings.
-I could not believe that this was true!

I asked the pastor what this meant, and he said that it was not entirely forbidden to pray for other people. I could pray for others in the last few minutes of the prayer meeting. But this was the time when they sang praise songs, so when could we pray for our fellow Christians?
There is only one thing to say about this - **control**, from one end to the other. What do they want to control? You, of course.
Why? So that you would not grow in Christ. You are thinking - this cannot be right. No Christian would try to stop other brothers and sisters from growing in the Lord, would they?
Unfortunately, this is the case in most churches. The spirit of control is powerful when it is allowed to take over.
It was not just me who was under control during the meetings. The people who did not receive prayer also suffered under this terrible control.

I have ministered to thousands of people during my time as a Christian and can testify to this as people come to be prayed for because they need it. It is as simple as that.

Many believers are at the baby stage in their lives. If they are willing to follow Christ, we ought to help those who are weak in the Spirit. Christians are tired because of the massive attack by Satan and his army of demons. The Bible says that those who are weak need to be encouraged and helped.
(1 Thessalonians 5:14)

Every Christian in the same situation should discern between God and Satan in what we hear from pastors, leaders, and other believers. We must daily work to become mature believers (Ephesians 4:13) so that we can take every thought captive in obedience to Christ. (2 Corinthians 10:5)

We need to be very careful as there is a strong warning in Matthew 7:21, about what we can expect when we build our kingdom.

Charitable aid work

One Sunday, as I sat in my usual place in church something, happened that caught my attention. The pastor spoke about aid work in a school in the Philippines, where the church was involved. We collected money towards buying school materials and other necessities they needed there. I felt that this was something for me, as my heart started beating fast even though I sat quite still.

I thought it was strange that I had never heard about this work before. It was exciting, and my first thought was that I wanted to get involved, not just give money. I often traveled to the Philippines, so it was not a great challenge for me.

I talked to another brother about this after the meeting, and he felt the same way. We took it up with the leadership, but all we got out of it was a bank account number to donate money.

Not long after this, a typhoon hit Manila, leaving thousands of thousands of people homeless, and many lost their lives. The church showed pictures of the mud mass inside the school. We went to the leaders again to offer our help. They refused us to help these poor people. It is shocking to think that several hundred children could not go to school and that there were people who wanted to help just sitting at home.

I know now why this happened. It was a smokescreen to show that the church was helping someone, somewhere.
This is nothing but terrible!

All Christians should get involved in charitable work, not just send money to a bank account. There is a great need in the world today for Spirit-filled Christians to get involved in reaching out to others who need our help. We stand in church and sing hallelujah but are not very interested in helping the needy.
-There is something very wrong with this picture.

Notes;

_____

_____

_____

_____

_____

_____

24

Notes;

_____

_____

_____

_____

_____

_____

_____

_____

_____

_____

_____

_____

CHAPTER 4

The spiritual world

It starts to open up

A short time after I met Jesus, the spiritual world began to open up. It all started with when the Lord showed me pictures of other believers. There was no doubt what the meaning of this was. It was only to obey and begin to pray. The result was a powerful intercession. To interpret what these pictures mean is something that takes time. Here you must stay close to the Lord, obeying what is coming, then understanding will come eventually.

Early one morning in Saron's Valley during the prayer meeting, I was suddenly pulled out into the spiritual world. I saw an approximately 100 feet tall demon which looked with a very angry and astonishing sight into the room where we prayed. Seconds later, I stood outside in front of him, and his whole body covered with long white hairs, and he had a royal crown of gold on his head, as well as a big wand with lots of decorations in his right hand. He was furious that I was in 'his' world. (The spiritual world)

He knocked down on the ground around me, a thick barbed wire to tie me up. He did not succeed because I used the name of Jesus.

At a later time, I saw the same demon again.

Aero

The Lord showed me how the demons are just waiting for humans to sin by pulling me out into the spiritual world. Once been there, I moved between thousands of demons. I also saw people down on earth.

While I moved between all these demons, it was just as if they were waiting for something. What I saw was when people sin, one or two demons flew down from the sky, and began to torment the one who had sinned. The people who the demons attacked, they walked on the street just as if they were heading somewhere. The first thing I thought about was: they sin in their thoughts because they did nothing but walking on a sidewalk.

In 2 Corinthians 10:5, there is a commandment on how to deal with our thoughts of life (spiritual warfare), but when you do not know the Lord, thoughts are just something you take for granted and think it should be like that. And when it comes to believers, unfortunately, there are a few who understand Satan's workplace, which is in our minds.

In Ephesians 2:2, Satan is called; The prince of the power of the air. It means; The satanic ruler over the spiritual area, which is termed 'the air.' In Greek, there are two words for air-aither that are associated with the word **ether** and **aer**.

This is the designation of the air layer immediately above the earth's surface. The first word **aiter** denotes the highest, thin atmosphere, and is not used for the atmosphere closest to the ground.

Satan and the Demons are very aware of their fall.
(Colossians 2:15)

Therefore, they work intensively 24/7 throughout the year. They never take a break to bother people.

They only do so to bring grief to the Father's heart.

One Sunday, when we arrived at the church, there was a considerable angel about 12 ft. high dressed up as a warrior outside the entrance. He just stood there, completely quiet. A little later that day, I saw a large number of demons flying over the church building.

-I did not speculate why I saw this.

These are just a few of many tours in the spiritual world.

The Lord will show you secrets from the heavenly. But it is you who must grab Him, spend time with Him according to His word. But unfortunately, most Christians do not get into this, as most people remain drinking milk. (Ephesians 4:14)

Python spirit

You are on your way to the church and are just feeling great. Last night's sleep was brilliant. The time has passed, the meeting can begin. It all starts with 3-4 worship songs, then some simple testimonies. Everything goes just perfect. The pastor begins to preach the word of God, and then it happens. Perhaps you are tempted to check Facebook, messages, or other similar things. Or you start to feel a bit tired, or maybe a small dose of no concentration appears. You may not respond to it, but this is where the chance is significant that it's a python spirit on the move.

A python spirit is a strangling spirit. He ensures that you get tired and has no concentration, and do whatever it takes to keep you from the content from the pulpit. When you accept this dull fatigue, this spirit continues to work on you until your focus is not ok anymore. The disaster is then a fact.

You left home happy and positive, now tired and no concentration. If you have become slightly unconcentrated at first, it is difficult to return to what you focused on earlier in the day.

A python spirit is a clever spirit. But if you are willing to learn, it is easy to learn how to reveal him. When you discern this demon, it also has no authority. Here, you can win, and the demon loses.

-It's all up to you.

Satan and the demons do not mind the word of God. But they are terrified that you will become the awesome giant that God has called you to be. The Bible says to resist the devil. (James 4:7)

When the Holy Spirit begins to reveal the word for you, when you start to understand and act on the word of God, Satan will come after you.

Satan does not accept that you are in the process of growing in the Word of God. He does not accept that you start to pray for sick, and at least he does not accept that you to begin to cast out demons. But how much shall you take from Satan?

-Nothing!

We stand firm on God's written word. The Lord gave us authority to trample on serpents and scorpions and over all the power of the enemy. (Luke 10:19)

The authority is ours; Now, we must learn to use it.

Does the Bible say anything about python spirits?
-Yes, it does.

Let us read in Acts 16, from verse 16-18;
V16 "Now it happened, as we went to prayer, that a certain slave girl possessed with **a spirit of divination** met us, who brought her masters much profit by fortune-telling.
V17 This girl followed Paul and us, and cried out, saying, **these men are the servants of the Most High God, who proclaim to us the way of salvation.**
V18 And this she did for many days. But Paul, greatly annoyed, turned and **said to the spirit,** I command you in the name of Jesus Christ to come out of her. And he came out that very hour."

In verse 16, we see that the girl had a spirit of divination. She was obsessed with a spirit that could predict. It could tell others in advance who the Apostles were. At the same time, the spirit prophesied that these men were God's servants who proclaimed the path of salvation to sinners. Here we see that demons like to speak a little about God and his work.
This slave girl followed them for several days to destroy their work for the Lord.

The woman prophesied - predicted the disciples who came and then had a spiritual revelation about this.

The King James Version of the Bible says, V16 "And it came to pass, as we went to prayer, a certain **damsel possessed** with a

spirit of divination met us, which brought her masters much gain by soothsaying."

Damsel means woman. Spirit of divination, let us go into the Greek and find out what this means; **Divination** in Greek does not only imply divination but Python. She was obsessed with a python spirit that is also a spirit of divination.

One of the areas in which the Python spirit operates is then divination. These include; Prophetic and Horoscopic. Horoscope, it's within the 'occult department.'
No matter where you move within the occult, you will meet a python spirit. There is nothing in the scriptures that tells us that demons work alone or work under a single task.

The purpose of the horoscope is
Increase the insight into a person's character, as well as tell about the future.
Have you fallen into temptation to receive a daily or weekly horoscope, the chances are that a python spirit has got a hold of you. You then need to repent to the Lord.

When you sin, you open the door to the spiritual realm. Then comes spirits, and they are demons.
-If we mess around with wrong spiritual things, wrong types of spirits come.

You have opened the door for these because you have contradicted God's written words. If the Lord says; You shall not seek - accept a horoscope, but you say; It's only in that magazine or newspaper that I bought. Then you have agreed with Satan, searching in the horoscope. At the same time, you have given authority to Satan and the demons to tie up.

Nor here is any guarantee that this demon will come alone. Neither Satan nor any of the demons, they go nowhere before you repent from sin and to Jesus. (Repent means stop doing, turn away from and to Christ)

-He alone can set you free.

Spiritual revelations

The Bible, the will of the Lord our God and commandments to humanity. We must fill ourselves with the word every single day. Daily we must spend time with the Lord, according to Matthew 6:6.

-Satan hates that you receive any spiritual revelations from the Lord.

Satan came to my home

One day I got a book called 'Get the stray dog out.'

It is a book about how Satan works systematically in many branches of religion, new age, spiritualism, occultism, philosophers, and more.

What might be most interesting was that when I started reading this book, I began to understand more about how Satan worked. Not only did I read what the author had written, but a spiritual understanding followed. There was little doubt that this author had revelations about what he wrote.

I read the book in one evening.

Along the way, a spirit of fear appeared in our house. It was simple to reveal, a cold gust of fear suddenly stood right in front of me while I was sitting on the couch. Furthermore, temptations beyond my imagination began to flow into my mind. Satan came as an angel of light and said I had to bow down to him.

-These were just some of the many experiences this evening.

Books that genuinely are of true spiritual nature, Satan is terrified for you to know to exist.

This world

We must accept the will of the Lord through His written words. We need all revelations from the Lord what is going on. If we get it, we will be able to reveal Satan and the demons, who work frantically to ruin everything you believe and do. The truth is; This world is a world of sin. Behind all sin are Satan and an ocean of demons.

The Bible cannot be more explicit; **Do not sin!**

All Christians must become very conscious and come into all that the Lord has for them.

"The thief (Satan) does not come except to steal, and to kill, and to destroy. **I have come that they may have life and that they may have it more abundantly.**" (John 10:10)

Why is not Christians 'there'?

Most of today's congregations are very good to mislead. They spend most of the time singing praise, coffee talk, and hanging after the pastor for all kinds of issues.

The Bible says we are in a war, and Satan is shooting on us with fiery darts. (Ephesians 6:12, 16)

Now it's time to slow down with the song practice and step up with the war studies.

You are a soldier of Christ
"Put on the **whole** armor of God, that you may be able to stand against the wiles of the devil." (Ephesians 6:11)

Spiritual understanding
You need to grow into spiritual knowledge, to understand how Satan is working to kill and destroy you. If you are one of those, who do not feel so 'troubled' in your Christian life or believe God has saved you for all these devilish attacks, if you believe this, then you must think again. We do not find this in the scripture.
Pick up your daily cross and follow the Lord and His commandments, then you'll see it starts to move in the spiritual realm.

Ephesians 6:1-9, is one of the places in the Bible that says you must live in constant sanctification. In verse 10-18, there is a commandment about to take on God's full armor. This scripture applies to all Christians, and nobody is exempted. Why? Because Satan will shoot at you with everything he has when you begin to obey the Lord.

The latter is how it is to be a Christian.

34

Notes;

CHAPTER 5

Voices

They are everywhere, the voices

It comes to the most amazing thing out of a 'brother or sisters'
mouth. Most of it is so religious and destructive that you have to
hold onto something when words are 'thrown' against you. The
Bible says we shall do everything in love, but I do not think that
so many people live in or have a revelation about what it means.

Shall you live in - after the following scripture, you must be one
who walks together with the Lord.

"Let all that you do be done with love." (1 Corinthians 16:14)

The Philippines

One day, someone in the church told me about a funeral that he
had attended in the Philippines. Most of the population in that
country are Catholics. When somebody dies, their tradition is to
balm the body.

The tradition is to have the open coffin inside the house, in the
kitchen, or the living room. This 'brother' conducted a Christian
work in the Philippines, so it was quite natural for us to talk
about things that happen in this country. His experiences and
understandings about this funeral were exceptional.

He said straight to me; Never go to a funeral in the Philippines.
They are dragging around this body a whole week, and they
drink alcohol, jump around this coffin screaming and shouting.
There are so many demons around these traditions, and they
agree with them all. If you go to a house or a place where they
have a funeral, you will be demonized and need deliverance afterward.
- "Okay," I answered and did not comment on the matter.

If this brother, which also had been a missionary for over 25
years, had been matured in Christ, then other words would have
come out of his mouth.
-We are in a war. We must all understand that who have chosen
to live a life for Jesus.

In Ephesians 6:12, we see who we have a war against. Further,
in verse 13, we read how to be standing to the next battle round.
Furthermore, the Bible says that we must come into a spiritual
understanding of what is happening around us in our daily lives.
We must grow out of the milk stage, and into the maturity in
Christ. (Ephesians 4:13-14)
-This must be taken seriously.

The funeral
A few years later, I was in a small village on an island south in
the Philippines, preaching the Gospel. Sickness was everywhere,
and the Lord did not fail with His promises regarding healing. A
little place that we have visited, we were invited to a funeral. We
arrived at the house of the deceased's family, and now I imme-

diately remembered the stay away propaganda from this 'brother' in the church at home.

-Did I worry about it? No.

The atmosphere among those who were in the house was sad, but it is normal when relatives and loved ones die. Approx. 10-12 people were in the living room, and the coffin was nicely parked right next to the sofa. It was the first time I saw a dead person in an open coffin. While we greeted everyone who was there, a thought came to me; Ask if anyone has any pain or illness that they are struggling with! "Yes Sir;" was my response. I started the survey, and in total, 8-9 people had pain and struggles.

-It was a time for healing.

Right next to the coffin, one by one, Jesus healed them. Everyone we prayed for, got a powerful demonstration of who Jesus is. The Lord can turn everything for His glory.

-By the way, I did not see any demons. Jesus I saw, but where the light is, the darkness must go. (Matthew 5:14-16)

Round 2 of the funeral

Philippine tradition says; When 40 days have passed, they celebrate it. I do not know what they're celebrating, but that's how it is.

A friend of mine, which is a pastor, was invited to the funeral to share the word of God. His entire congregation stood up for the occasion. When we arrived, the song of praise was already well underway.

While this was happening, the Lord shows me a lady whom He wanted to do something with. A little song of praise is not in the way, so I went to her and said, come with me over to the other side to the fence, and I'll pray for you.
I laid my hand on her right ear and prayed in the name of Jesus. The presence of the Lord appeared, and she cried like never before. All the pain in her ear disappeared.

Later she told me that for years, she had gone to several different doctors and hospitals. They had never been able to figure out what was wrong with her ear. A lot of different prescriptions were all that came out of it. But Jehovah Rapha, the Lord our Healer (Exodus 15:26) knew what was wrong with her ear.
-The Lord heals when we lay hands on the sick. (Mark 16:18)

A guy showed up, and he, for sure, did not look good. He told me that he had fallen from a 30-ft. High coconut tree a long time ago. To survive that kind of fall is a miracle itself. The back pain he had was almost indescribable. He was quite crooked in his back and smiling; I think it was a long time ago he had experienced.
-I laid my hand on the bottom of his back. While I prayed, he was reticent and just staring to the ground. I have seen this many times before, a fairly common reaction when the Lord is on the move. The pain disappeared, and the smile began to come back.
-Jesus Christ is the healer, and He loves to heal.

If we are obedient to the written word of God, the Lord is never late to keep His promises.

These signs shall follow for those who believe; Who are those who believe? All the believers that believe and act on it. It follows you: it does not go ahead of you. Your faith must be activated. (Mark 16:17-18)
-You believe you act, then it happens. It is written.

If God tells me so

When you challenge other believers about healing or go out in the world with the Lord's Gospel, they will confront with statements like this; If it is God's will, if God tells me to go, I will go. Or; In God's time, I will do it.

He has already said that in the Bible. His own written words - to you and me.
-What are we waiting for?
In John 1:1 it says; The Word is God. There you see. The written word, the Bible, is God who speaks to us. If God says something in the Bible, **it is already spoken to us and revealed to us**.
It means in all simplicity; You have been given a commandment for you to accomplish.
-What are you waiting for?

Not before God says it

One day I had a conversation with one of the elders in the church about leaving the church. It came as a bomb what he had to say. If God says you are going to sign out, you can opt-out, not before!
It was a very controlling way to tell me how to do it, and it did not make any sense to me.

It took a while before we left the church, but I did not wait for the Lord's speech. The written word in the Bible was enough for me.

We read in 2 Corinthians 6:14 that no Christian should agree with unbelief.

Where the infidelity is, there is also control.

-It was enough of both in that place.

I did not make any sense

From the day I was saved, I began to fill myself with the word of God. There was a hunger within me that only God's Word could satisfy. At that time, I worked as a truck driver emptying garbage in the city of Oslo. It was a governmental company, and the working days were not as 'effective' as they should have been. Many places around the capital, you could see yellow garbage trucks that were parked both here and there long before and after lunch. There was enough time to do what we all have to do every single day. Namely; To fill ourselves with the written Word of God.

"This Book of the Law shall not depart from your mouth, but you shall meditate on it day and night, that you may observe to do according to all that is written in it. For then you will make your way prosperous, and then you will have good success." (Joshua 1:8)

"But his delight is in the law of the Lord, and in His law he meditates day and night. He shall be like a tree planted by the rivers of water, that brings forth its fruit in its season.

Whose leaf also shall not wither, and whatever he does shall prosper." (Psalm 1:2-3)

I understood quite early that the mission commandment described in Mark 16:15; It is a commandment from the Lord to all believers. It is not only the Evangelist who shall be going out into the whole world but the entire body of Christ.

Eventually, in the church, I began to put my finger on this, and the resistance I got I did not expect to get from the congregation. But this was just the beginning of learning how demonic spirits work. Countless times it was thrown at me; The Bible is a thick book, and you do not see the forest for all the trees. It's not just about the mission commandment, and not everyone is going to do it. We are not all evangelists. Etc, etc.

It is quite interesting that God, through His written word, the Bible has an entirely different opinion of the matter. The word Evangelist denotes one that conveys a good message. The good news of Jesus' crucifixion and the resurrection, we shall all bear.

Listen; Do the work of an evangelist, fulfill your ministry. (2 Timothy 4:5)

The commandment of Christ to all Christians
You shall love your neighbor as yourself.
(Matthew 22:39 - Romans 13:9)

You shall love the Lord your God with all your heart, with all your soul, and with all your mind. (Matthew 22:37)

Go into all the world and preach the Gospel to every creature. (Mark 16:15)

For the whole law is fulfilled in one commandment; You shall love your neighbor as yourself! (Galatians 5:14)

Jesus died for all sinners

Jesus chose you and me to do the job. We are to cast out demons, proclaim the kingdom of God, and heal the sick in the name of Jesus. We are all called to be Kingdom demonstrators, and we shall reach out our hands to a dying world. The world where it lives hordes of people who can't afford either the daily meals, the doctor, nor the dentist. The need is unbelievably high. More than 20000 children die of hunger and illness every single day, and everyone who dies every day **is all children of God**.

Jesus came to save the world (John 3:17), and how can people be saved? It is you and I who shall go out and preach the gospel to every sinner for repentance. To all the sinners who are on their way to eternal death. (Romans 6:23)
We shall draw them out of the way to eternal destruction and to eternal salvation with Jesus Christ. As you do this, lay your hands on the sick and help the fatherless and widows.

The poor are very close to the Lord, and He waits for us to start using our hands to reach out to the needy. There is only one cure for all sorts of diseases; It is you and your hands together with the mighty name of Jesus Christ. When you believe and act on God's commandment in the Bible. (Mark 16:18)

Why do you not go? Why do you not believe it?

-You do not go because you do not want to.

All the time there are statements like this;

-I do not have 'that' in my heart.

-I do not have it on my mind.

-The Lord has not told me that.

This way of talking from someone who proclaims to be a believer belongs in a crossword competition, not in a believer's faith, mind, and actions.

The Bible says; Do not trust your feelings.

Will God speak through your feelings?

Yes. Spending time with the Lord (Matthew 6:6) be rooted in His word and obey what He says. Doing this will make you sensitive to hear the voice of God.

"I will open my mouth in a parable; I will utter dark sayings of old." (Psalm 78:2)

This world says; Follow your heart

After your heart, will be; Looking for what's right, at the moment, whether it's correct.

-We cast the caution and the conscience to the wind. As well as pursue your last whim and wishes. This is the philosophy of new age gurus, self-help seminars, and romantic pop singers.

We follow God's written word, the Bible.

44

The Bible says

"He who trusts in his own heart is a fool, but whoever walks wisely will be delivered." (Proverbs 28:26)

It is the written Word of God that applies.
-Nothing else is more important.

What God says through the scripture is the most important thing. Not your feelings.
How can we see that your feelings are correct or incorrect?
When they are not in line with God's written words, they are wrong. Either we believe in God's word and act on it, or we do not believe it. If we do not believe, we are an unbeliever.

The Spirit is coming

Every day, every week, we must chase for the biblical truth.
Daily we must meditate on the word of God.
Every single day, we must seek the Lord in the quiet.
(Matthew 6:6)
We must be rooted in the word to remain in all the struggles against Satan and the demons. (Ephesians 6:13)
The most prominent critic of your own Ministry must become yourself.

Satan is sitting on the first row in the church every Sunday. He is looking for someone to devour. (1 Peter 5:8)
Do you give the devil place in your statements and ways, to your brothers and sisters? (Ephesians 4:27)
Do you do all things in love? (1 Corinthians 16:14)

Here is an example

It was a Sunday, just before it all started in the church. A 'brother' and I had a pleasant conversation down by the altar, and the conversation had no specific subject. Suddenly it came from him; We must do what the pastor says.

-Excuse me, what did you say?

We must not run around and do everything ourselves, but we must do what the pastor says he replied.

No, we shall not, I replied. We shall relate to Jesus, and His written words The Bible.

No pastor shall decide what to do. To submit to this kind of control is wrong.

And here comes the point;

The church - congregation today has very little spiritual understanding. All Christians must come to maturity with the Lord. (Ephesians 4:13)

If we do not do this, we are tossed to and fro and carried about with every wind of doctrine, by the trickery men. (Ephesians 4:14)

If you speak something that is not by the scripture, you agree with untruths, and there you find the whole league of demons, plus the one who walks around like a roaring lion and seeks someone to devour.

If you accept what they bring, they will work through you as a believer - more info in Hebrews 5:14.

Everyone shall function in distinguishing between spirits. There are not just someone 'special' selected who will do this.

It is crucial to get an understanding of how Satan shoots his burning arrows on us Christians, through other believers, unsaved, and to our minds. We must become specialists to take every thought into captivity, under obedience to Christ. Take them captive before they give birth to sin.
(2 Corinthians 10:5 - James 1:15)

"Nor give place to the devil." (Ephesians 4:27)

There are only truths and untruths. Therefore, the Lord has given us the Bible and the Holy Spirit. (1 John 4:6 - John 14:6)

Speak as God's word says. Your words are spiritual
"If anyone speaks, let him speak as the oracles (revelations) of God. If anyone ministers, let him do it as with the ability which God supplies, that in all things God may be glorified through Jesus Christ, to whom belong the glory and the dominion forever and ever. Amen." (1 Peter 4:11)

Let no corrupt word proceed out of your mouth.
(Ephesians 4:29)

The boat trip
One weekend, we went on a boat trip to Kiel - Germany, with some of the church members. It was at the end of our membership, and we were on our way out of the church. I remember well during the dinner; I told them we were going to opt-out. -Then it came; If you leave the church, you will become fatherless and are on your own.

‹‹What kind of talk was this? I did not intend to become a Buddhist or Muslim.››

These kinds of statements are, unfortunately, many 'Christians' who allow **themselves** to pronounce.
-A perfect example of being judged right into darkness.

Neither the pastor nor the church should be associated with the following scripture;
"Do not **call** (act as if) anyone on earth your father, for One is your Father, He who is in heaven." (Matthew 23:9)

"I will not leave you orphans; I will come to you." (John 14:18)

It is the Lord we shall relate to, not a pastor and the church.
-Draw near to God, and He will draw near to you. (James 4:8)

What is coming out of your mouth? What is your spirit filled with?
The Bible says; If anyone speaks, let him speak as the oracles (only revelations) of God. (1 Peter 4:11)

The Bible says further in James 3:5;
"Even so the tongue is a little member and boasts great things. See how great a forest a little fire kindles!"

If we fill ourselves with what is negative, it creates negativity. If we fill ourselves with the Word of God, we speak what the word of God says.

48

The Holy Ghost creates what the word says. God's word is created in our lives and circumstances. The positive become created.

-**Everything God creates is positive**.

Notes;

_____

_____

_____

_____

_____

_____

_____

_____

_____

_____

CHAPTER 6

When you go in agreement with today's church

Today's churches rely too much on feelings and experiences. Experiences of a spiritual character; Shaking, trembling, loud cries, and prophetic words are what we seek. We want God's attention, but it should be as <u>we</u> want it. Do we not have the right' experiences,' we chase after those until we think we get them.
This draws us away from God and His written Word.

It's a wonderful promise in Matthew 6:6, why not believe that this is for you? It is you who must take the job in the secret closet to seek God, as the scripture says. Stop running after others that you 'think' has received something from the Lord at all times, or 'have the anointing.'

When you have people around you who are functioning in the prophetic, you'll recognize him right away when you are distinguishing between spirits. Many people who operate in the prophetic are not prophetic at all. A carnal behavior with a fleshly 'experience' is what is served. The Lord, our God, is a sober God and have no delight in that we are dragged around by every wind of doctrine. (Ephesians 4:14)

50

If you go in agreement with a church that does not have any plans to go into the entire world with the Gospel, make disciples out there, cast out demons and heal the sick, then you have gone in agreement with the unbelievers.

-The Word unbeliever means in all simplicity; Disobedient to God.

Doubt

The religious doubt is a doubt on God himself. Although it is written, we doubt. The first humans lived in faith and trust in their creator. But it was planted a seed in their minds from the enemy. Has God indeed said: you shall not eat of every tree of the garden? (Genesis 3:1)

Instead of rejecting the doubts, they chose it. The assessment capability got a negative sign and a tendency to doubt and disbelief. After the fall, there is, in human nature, an innate doubt in God, fear, and unwillingness against Him.

"Because the carnal mind is enmity against God; for it is not subject to the law of God, nor indeed can be." (Romans 8:7)

Doubts in prayer and scripture are doubt in God's power

The Bible says, Whoever doubts when he prays does not hold on to God's promises and looks like a wave of the sea, being tossed by the wind. (James 1:6)

If we doubt, we must not expect to get anything from the Lord. (James 1:7-8)

Believers doubt - one of Satan's weapons against the believers to lead them to apostasy
You think; That you do not have what it takes or has the gift of healing to pray for the sick. You doubt, and it leads to disbelief.

It is written
"But He was wounded for our transgressions; He was bruised for our iniquities; the chastisement for our peace was upon Him, and by His stripes we are healed." (Isaiah 53:5)

"Who Himself bore our sins in His own body on the tree, that we, having died to sins, might live for righteousness - by whose stripes you were healed." (1 Peter 2:24)

Now you obey the commandment in Mark 16:15-18. If you have faith as a mustard seed, you can move mountains.
(Matthew 17:20)

If you do not believe, there is no doubt that this is disbelief.

God must be grasped in faith. (Hebrews 11:1)

The way out of doubt.
God's goodness is the only thing that can overcome this attitude by man. Here we must get really into God's presence and seek the Lord.

-God's Word, we must ponder every single day. (Joshua 1:8)

-Our faith must be build up. (Romans 10:17)

The way of thinking and speculations does not lead to freedom of doubt. No one can think their way out of the doubt or come to faith with reasonable evidence and arguments.

Doubts are resolved by faith is the substance of things hoped for, the evidence of things not seen. (Hebrews 11:1)

When God's Word and Spirit creates faith in the human heart, it defeats the doubt by the Spirit's conviction.

Note; The pastor is not mentioned in the subsequent passage; The Holy Spirit will teach you all things. (John 14:26)

If you act on the Word, something happens. Heaven was opened for you by the beautiful work that Jesus did on Calvary. If you do not act on the Word of God, the Holy Spirit will not be able to teach you much, and it all becomes dead. (James 2:26)

Disbelief

A negative attitude among the people toward God and a denial of God's written Word.

"Do not be unequally yoked together with unbelievers. For what fellowship has righteousness with lawlessness? And what communion has light with darkness?" (2 Corinthians 6:14)

Believers use their disbelief to justify themselves, through the scriptures above God and you.

Example 1, pray for sick

They do not want to pray for the sick. They are healthy themselves, are selfish above the sick. They say they do not have the grace to pray for the sick and that not everyone shall do it. You might be new to the road with the Lord or have a long time been in a congregation practicing this kind of unbelief. No matter what, the answer is always in the Bible.

It is written
They will lay hands on the sick, and they will recover.
(Mark 16:18)
-Who are those who believe? All those who believe!
(Mark 16:17)

Here the scripture says the opposite of the example above. The unbelievers (those who are disobedient to the Lord) the Bible clearly states that we shall not be unequally yoked with.
(2 Corinthians 6:14)

Read, meditate, believe and act only on God's written words
"And you shall know the truth, and the truth shall make you free." (John 8:32)

Example 2; The Mission Commandment
They do not want to go out and preach the Gospel; They are busy with everything else. They say it is the evangelist who is going to go out and preach the Gospel. It is the pastor's task to send out the workers to harvest. The Bible is a thick book, so there are many 'different' tasks. Therefore, not all shall 'go' to preach and proclaim the Gospel. My 'call' is in the song of praise, the 'call' of the others is in the praise team, and the third's 'call' is in child ministry. And the latter says he will work

six days, and the seventh he will rest. Then he cannot go to 'church' because it is written.

These statements are coming all the time, proclaimed from the sidelines. There is no cover for this infidelity in the Bible. All these bring forth is more disbelief and breakdown to the body of Christ.

"Go therefore and make disciples of all the nations, baptizing them in the name of the Father and of the Son and the Holy Spirit, teaching them to observe all things that I have command-ed you; and lo, I am with you always, even to the end of age." (Matthew 28:19-20)

"And He said to them, go into all the world and preach the gospel to every creature." (Mark 16:15)
-Here we see that everyone is going to proclaim the Gospel of Jesus Christ.

The praise team, the Shepard, and the child ministry is the min-istry of help. (1 Corinthians 12:28)
-We help where we can, but this work does not exceed the mis-sion commandment.

As Christians, we have a great responsibility for God's written Word. On your judgment day, you will stand before the God of love and wrath. (Hebrews 9:27)
Are you someone who has lived a life like an infidel? (Galatians 5:19-21 - Revelation 21:8)
-We must choose our fellowship with care.

Get out of your boat

They sat in the boat, Jesus said; See you on the other side. He did not plan to take the boat with them. Jesus had other plans. He came later.

The Bible says that Peter walked on water.
It is, by definition, impossible for a human being to walk on water. Peter did not walk on water. It was just as impossible then as it is now 2000 years later. Peter walked on **God's promise** that he could come to Jesus on the sea. As a result, Peter had to take that big step over the boat rip, first one leg then the other. Peter knew that he could not walk on water. But Jesus said **come,** and Peter chose to trust Jesus and His promise, not his understanding. As a result, Peter could walk on water.

And how is it with you? Are you comfortable in your safe boat? You may be sitting in the middle of where it swings, at least. Then it's time and not thinking of what kind of spiritual gifts you have or what type of call you have, dear to act on God's Word instead. Jesus has called you out among people, for and preaching the Gospel of the crucified Christ. Get out of your boat and dare to believe God's written Word the Bible. Dare to believe that training will be provided while you are at work. Dare to believe that signs and wonders will flow out of you, to those who need it.
-Now you believe, now you act, Jesus is waiting out there.

We'll be seated.
It's the most Christians motto. We sit and ask the Lord to send the people into the churches of ours. We pray and believe that it

is the Lord who builds His church, then He may send the lost sheep into the house of our church, so we can take two steps forward and greet them. But only 2 hours on Sunday, otherwise we're closed.

-This has nothing to do with the truth.

The altar call

The pastor preaches according to today's schedule, it runs like on tracts, just like he has made it. Then something happens. The music begins, and a custom-made song comes. Everyone is told to bow their heads and not look up. Then the pastor makes the "alter call." People receive an offer to accept Jesus as their Lord and Savior.

The Bible says; The whole heavens rejoice over a sinner who repents! (Luke 15:7, 10)

-And we are told to close our eyes, bow our heads and not see?

Jesus died for all sinners.

People can never repent from sin if they do not know what sin is and what the Bible says about sin and repentance. That is what is needed to be preached to sinners, for repentance. When a sinner understands that he has violated God's laws and is guilty of hell's fire, one can harvest. Not before.

Why sink when you can float

When Peter had walked some steps on the water, he saw the great storm coming. Then he began to sink. Peter immediately called for help from Jesus. The arm of our Lord and Savior was

not late to seize him. Listen to what Jesus says about this; O you
of little faith, why did you doubt?

What about you, do you doubt what Jesus tells you to do? If you
do, you will sink and become an easy swap for Satan and the
demons. Do you believe and stand firmly on God's written
Word, you will not sink. The Lord's promises are for you and
me for us to succeed in what we do.

Trust the Lord's promises

As Christians, we need to rely on what the Scriptures say. If it is
in the Bible, it is from the Lord; Then, it is obvious to us. The
written Word of God is the same as if the Lord stands next to
you as a visible person and speaks to you.

The Bible says

"In the beginning, was the Word, and the Word was with God,
and the Word was God." (John 1:1)

-All scripture is given by inspiration of God. (2 Timothy 3:16)

Disobedience to the Mission Commandment

One day, the phone rang. It was a 'brother' that I had known for
a few years. He had a revelation that he wanted me to understand. He knew that I was the one who is out in the world and
preaching the Gospel. What he wanted to say was very important to him, and he stammered and harked before he started shar-
ing this 'revelation.'

There was a powerful ministry somewhere in Africa, which
traveled around and preached the Gospel, prayed for the sick,
and cast out demons. This 'pastor' had raised money from the
audience the places he had been around and preached. This had

resulted that the Lord had taken him out of ministry for a few years. This 'brother's revelation was the money offer. He tried everything he could to make me understand how important it is not doing this among the poor, and instead rely on the Lord when it comes to the finances.

-He was very sincere in his speech.

But if he had been as sincere with the Lord himself, he had begun to obey the mission commandment instead.

You are deceiving yourself when you do not. Then the Holy Spirit may not train you up into the necessary things to execute the commandment. Jesus' disciples, they received training at work and not in the church building. Part 2 of my answer is; When you are in the poor parts of the world when you stand before the fatherless, and you see how the Lord and His power work through you, you will experience something wonderful; To be Jesus' love among the least. Then you will never ask for financial support among them to your ministry. It will be a typical day at work, and the only thing you think of when you are among the least is to give.

Greater than all the gifts of the Spirit are love.
(1 Corinthians 13)

The spiritual side
The church needs to understand that it is a substantial spiritual side of the Bible. The physical world cannot be separated from the spiritual world. Behind every thought behind each word, it is a spirit. All Christians must come into an understanding of this. There is a spiritual confusion around the world today, and the church is out of course. Some have understood it, but most do

not. We are only concerned with what is happening within the four walls of the congregation. There is a little or no revelation about why Jesus died on the cross. Had it been, everything had been entirely different. The world is overflowing with sin, and they all wait that someone will come and demonstrate the kingdom of God. This is through the power of the Spirit, and not long, awful sermons.

"For the kingdom of God is not in word but in power."
(1 Corinthians 4:20)

You cannot blame the church or the pastor

There have been many excuses here. The pastor is not good enough; The church is not good enough. But the question is; Are you good enough? The responsibility for Christ is ours alone. Do you want to grow in Jesus? Get into the world and be the giant God has called you to be. Jesus is your rescue; You must be solely responsible for Him. Do you want to live victoriously with Him, everything must be laid down for Him.

Lukewarmness

If you are a lukewarm Christian and cruising around in your bubble, maybe it's interesting to pay attention to the following scripture;

"So then, because you are lukewarm and neither cold nor hot, I will vomit you out of My mouth." (Revelation 3:16)

If you are in this category, the next question is for you; **Are you born again?**

Notes;

_____

_____

_____

_____

_____

_____

_____

_____

_____

_____

_____

_____

CHAPTER 7

Religious spirits

It is of utmost importance that it is the Lord, who is the source
of your knowledge when it comes to how Satan and the demons
are working to destroy and control people. What is written about
the subject in this book, take it along your way.
It's not just how darkness works against you as a person, but
your struggle will also be from other people who are then under
the same conditions.

Let me explain how we can say there are religious spirits.

Satan's thoughts to the mind.
There are two different ways dark spiritual forces can rule us.
One is Satan, who sends thoughts to your mind, for making you
obey what he says to you.
He wants you to be his disciple in everything you take for you -
a life of sin and pleasure, a life without God and His revelations.
Satan has nothing against that you are using any of your time
with the Lord because he knows that he cannot erase God from
your heart.
Therefore, he will use the thoughts of the mind to destroy all
that you stand in with the Lord.

The other is demons.

Demons that intake people and get them to act on what they want. I will not address the theme of demons here, but I will refer to Scripture to illustrate the difference between Satan and demons. It is of utmost importance that you are not satisfied with what is written here, but continue in your quest for the Lord. He wants to show you and train you up in the distinguishing between spirits.

Listen;

"Now it happened, as we went to prayer, that a certain slave girl possessed with a spirit of divination met us, who brought her masters much profit by fortune-telling. This girl followed Paul and us, and cried out, saying, these men are the servants of the Most High God, who proclaim to us the way of salvation."
(Acts 16:16-17)

A demon who gets access to us, he gets access to our thoughts, our mouth and disturbs what comes into our ears. The believer is bound in several areas of his life and becomes a messenger for demons. He pronounces negative things; He is negative in his actions and becomes one that prevents the kingdom of God to grow. Like the woman in Acts 16:16-17, which is influenced by a Python spirit.

When Peter opposed Calvary's work, we see a different appearance than the slave girl with the spirit of divination. He had walked with Jesus for a few years and knew who He was. Jesus had told the disciples that He had to suffer and crucified. But in

Matthew, we see that Peter suddenly opposed the entire recon-
ciliation work that would take place at Calvary.
-He begins to speak out against what his master came to earth
for. Namely, the task at Calvary.

Jesus predicts his death and resurrection, but Peter means something completely different

"From that time Jesus began to show to His disciples that He
must got to Jerusalem, and suffer many things from the elders
and chief priests and scribes, and be killed, and be raised the
third day. Then Peter took Him aside and began to rebuke Him,
saying, far be it from You, Lord; this shall not happen to You!
But He turned and said to Peter, get behind Me Satan! You are
an offense to Me, for you are not mindful of the things of God,
but the things of men." (Matthew 16:21-23)

We attend churches, participate in cell groups, and we have so-
called fellowship with others. But do we understand how we are
held down by religious spirits in these gatherings? Do we know
how Satan uses the Scripture, through other believers to strike
you? So hard - that you never get into man's maturity in Christ.

Have you ever really entered what the Lord has for you?
You may feel unsatisfied. Maybe you think that it is hard to be a
Christian. You may wonder why there is no action at the Christ-
ian congregations you participate in. Then you have felt correct.
The religious demons are working hard throughout your life and
through other believers. All of these hinder you in God's work.

-It's time to take a new stance in your Christian life. Who are you going to have fellowship with, and shall you now start to obey God's written commandments in the Bible?

I have chosen to bring along some of my own experiences so that you can come to a greater understanding of how the religious works through those you least know. They will use all the 'tricks' that originated in the 'black book' so that you will not come into the position the Lord wants you to be.

The letter kills

When I decided to go to the Philippines, I shared with several 'brothers' that I looked very much forward to traveling. There, I should be the love of Christ among the least, pray for the sick and proclaim the gospel. Several times the following was thrown in my face; When you raise people from wheelchairs, then you can come and tell us.

This came from Christians who believe they are matured in the Lord, and on top of it all, they call themselves leaders.

-Jealousy and religious demons are what is flowing out of these "leaders."

Why are Christians envious?

Simply because they think that they have what it takes, but they are not willing to pay the price to go with the gospel. They live in the middle of their religious prison and do not accept that others are anything but what they are. This has nothing to do with the fruits of the Spirit, as the Bible describes in Galatians 5.

In the same chapter, we read about the fruit of the flesh. Envy is a fruit of the flesh. (Galatians 5:19-21)

Controlling spirits are the answer. Controlling spirits are allowed to flow freely out of the one who speaks down to you, and tries to hold you down. This is hard for anyone who has decided to do something for the Lord.

If you recognize yourself here, there are two things to say; Believe Matthew 12:33, and act on 2 Corinthians 6:14.

For out of the abundance of the heart, the mouth speaks. (Matthew 12:34)

"Love suffers long and is kind; **love does not envy**; love does not parade itself, is not puffed up." (1 Corinthians 13:4)

The fruit of the Spirit is love, joy, peace, longsuffering, kindness, goodness, faithfulness, gentleness, self-control. (Galatians 5:22)

If we live in the Spirit, let us also walk in the Spirit. (Galatians 5:25)

Those who are envy shall not inherit the Kingdom of God. (Galatians 5:20-21)

We must grab ourselves and go through our lives. Self-examination is something all Christians must live in.

-Daily we must live in the destruction of ourselves.

"He must increase, but I must decrease." (John 3:30)

It is very serious about being a Christian, for we are all responsible for the Lord with our lives and actions.

-God resists the proud but gives grace to the humble.
(James 4:6)

The Bible says
Love the Lord your God with all your heart.
(Matthew 22:37 - Luke 10:27)
Love your neighbor as yourself. (Matthew 22:39 - Romans 13:9)
Go and preach the gospel and make disciples.
(Matthew 28:19-20 - Mark 16:15)

The religious spirits work intensely against you to keep you going on the same track again and again. You become spiritually
bound in many areas of your life. You get used to moving
around the way you are bound. Therefore, we all must enter into
maturity in Christ. (Ephesians 4:13)
If not, you will be like children tossed to and fro and carried
about with every wind of doctrine, by the trickery of men, in the
cunning craftiness of deceitful plotting.

**They speak most of the time down to you like a burdensome
law that hangs over you.**

Jesus said, Take my **yoke** on you and learn from Me.
(Matthew 11:29)
Let's look at the Greek word yoke. Yoke is Zugos in Greek, and
it means: **join**. That means that whatever Jesus has for you, you
can carry.

-Start be a doer of the word, and do not let others destroy your journey with the Lord.

If you are in a congregation, a cell group, or participate in something with people who have controlling demons, you always leave with a heavy veil hanging over you.
Do you recognize yourself here, then cut them out and leave them alone. You are too important for the Lord in the work which He has for you. Do not waste your time on people who pretend to be something they have never been or will ever be.

The Spirit gives life
Therefore, the living gospel of Christ Jesus must be proclaimed to every creature. If you go, the Holy Ghost will teach you all things. (John 14:26)
If you do not want to go, what do you expect the Holy Ghost will teach you?

Bound
Your prayer life - how is it? Is it gentle and kind, or is there any action in it? Just as in your home as in prayer meetings, the religious demons are working intensely, so that you will never enter the prayer life that the Lord wants you to have.

Jesus teaches the disciples to pray in Luke 11:1-13.
In verse 8, it is a significant word, and that is **persistence**. Let us read the Scripture: "I say to you, though he will not rise and give to him because he is his friend, yet because of his **persistence** he will rise and give him as many as he needs."

Persistence in Greek means **shameless**. He got his loaves just because of his persistence. (Shameless)

How about your prayer life, are you shameless in prayer in front of the Lord?

How to reveal religious spirits in other believers?
If you reveal them, it depends on how spiritually mature you are. Very often, they are not interested in doing anything for the Lord but in justifying themselves throughout the time, telling you what to do and not to do according to a lot of scriptures. This is easy and transparent because they will never speak to you for lifting you in understanding in God's word, or your faith. They hate the fact that you have decided to preach the gospel of Jesus Christ, heal the sick, and cast out the demons.
-Open your spiritual eyes, for so real, is the world of the spirit.

It always comes; The Scripture says we cannot.
It always comes; The Scripture says we shall not.
Never will it come; The Scripture says we can.
Very often; You must not be so 'hard' when you preach.

They always speak down to the scriptures so that you do enter or understand what the Lord has for you.

They are usually sad in their faces, and smiling is rare. When a religious spirit grabs you, they do what they can to control you. No joy at all, everything is going like on rails according to them and their arrangements. They work intensely in the church and cell groups, and if there are any sick people present in the fellowship, they often get thrown in their faces on the way out: 'we' will pray for you. The fruit of their sanctification shows itself.

- When this behavior is "served" to you, there's a small sentence you might consider; **No thanks**.

You may have a brother or sister in the Lord, and at times there are statements like;
We must be careful not to brag about ourselves.
We must not boast of what we give to others.
We must not boast of what we do for the Lord.
We must be careful not to offend anyone.
We must not be haughty.
You must not be so direct!

It's coming 'we must' all the time. It's the main thing you will recognize it. It does not sanctify at all in your heart. Everything just feels miserable when you are or have been with these controlling religious officers. Controllers who just want to talk down to you, only to justify themselves and their ways. They are quick to tell you not to trust your feelings because it's written. You rarely find a religious who at all understands anything about distinguishes between spirits. Opinions about it most likely they have, but you will experience the fruit of it quickly.
-Their controlling statements and feelings is the game they play all the time.

This kind of behavior from a religious 'Christian, a pastor, or his leadership kills the present plans and will of the Holy Ghost right away.

Do you have such 'believers' around you as described here, just go another way. Because they will continue to speak a little positive to you then to hammer you down, only for you to stay 'there.' This is a highly abnormal Christian life, according to God's written Word.

-Believe and act on 2 Corinthians 6:14. This Scripture also speaks about unbelieving Christians. Unbelief means in all simplicity; **Disobedient to God**.

Even easier explained

Galatians 5:19-21 refer to the acts of the flesh. Do you see any of this in the ones you have around you, you understand that it's just to stay away. At the end of verse 21, it is written; Those who practice such things will not inherit the kingdom of God. The works of the flesh bring death and corruption into your life. You must have the fruit of the Spirit in your own life, and a similar fellowship is what you need. (Galatians 5:22-26)

We relate only to God's written Word, the Bible. Not to any other believer.

The Bible says, "For My yoke is easy and My burden is light." (Matthew 11:30)

Traditions

We have traditions in and for everything weird. This is a door that Satan uses to make strongholds in people.

Human traditions are not something the Lord has pleasure in

"Beware lest anyone cheat you through philosophy and empty deceit, according to the tradition of men, according to the basic principles of the world, and not according to Christ."
(Colossians 2:8)

The Lord does not want us to be tied up by human traditions. But only get our doctrines through His written Word.

Traditions in the Philippines
In the fall of 2013, there was an earthquake of 7.2 on Richter's scale on the island of Bohol-Philippines. Major injuries occurred everywhere, and many people died. It is clear that this does something to the people, and the fear is spreading among the citizens. They cry for a savior, but most of them are not rooted in the word of God. The Catholic Church spread out to the people that it was Saint Nino who had stopped the earthquake.
(Saint Nino: an idol in the eyes of the Lord)
What do the authorities do on the island after this 'revelation' that Saint Nino was the rescue? They introduce an annual day off at all public schools and celebrate that Saint Nino stopped the earthquake. Here you see a tradition introduced, and it is not in harmony with God's written Word.
-A covenant with Satan is what has been signed.

All saint's day
All saint's day is a day you can never imagine if you have not experienced it in the Philippines. Thousands of people travel to the cemeteries, where there is a disco, dance, barbecue, and al-

cohol are floating all over the place. Of course, the Catholic priesthood is there to keep what they call God's service. They sprinkle holy water on the people, walking back and forth on the tombs and pray to the dead. Virgin Mary is the leader of these people. Hail Mary, Mother of God, Catholics pray all the time. They are entirely drunk in their idolatry.

-This is a spiritual disorder and has nothing to do with Jesus Christ at all.

We do not pray to the dead, and Virgin Mary cannot help one soul here on earth or after they have died. They do not understand this and do not want to understand either. They have more faith in the words of the priest and the traditions of the country than in God's written word, the Bible. It's all straightforward; Not one idol worshipper will ever enter the gates of heaven. (Revelation 21:8)

Do you agree with this tradition of idolatry, eternal damnation in the lake of fire awaits.

-Repentance from this sin is the only thing the Lord accepts.

The Bible says
This book of the Law shall not depart from your mouth, but you shall meditate in it day and night. (Joshua 1:8 - Psalm 1:2)

In this case, out with the priest, and in with the truth, which is the word of God. Sixty-six books gathered in one bind to humanity. For you to have God, Himself revealed to you. (2 Timothy 3:16 - John 14:26)

"Jesus Christ is the same yesterday, today, and forever."
(Hebrews 13:8)

Fiesta

One week a year, in every barangay (small towns) there is a party they call for a fiesta. Then the marketplace is full of sellers who come from far away to sell all kinds of things. At one of the fiesta, we were in a city called Valencia in Bohol-Philippines. We had brought with us our banners since evangelism was on our program. The Catholic Church is not on the lazy side in a week like this. Together with the authorities, they had designed a lot of posters with a tribute to Saint Nino. These posters were hung up around the entire city.
You only need to know one Bible verse to understand that this Fiesta is one great idol.

Exodus 20:4-6 tells all about this matter.
It's a street dance, and the whole city is boiling. The alcohol is flooding, and the Catholic church is filled to the rim all day. Jesus Christ is nothing but a little child that Virgin Mary holds in her arms. They think Mary is God's mother.
-What a lie.
Spiritually, it is hard to proclaim Jesus in such a place. They have agreed with Satan to worship him through an idol. But we were about to proclaim the real Christ, and He never fails and many miracles we experienced that the Lord did this day.

The food

It was close to Christmas Eve, and my family would celebrate Christmas together. We were visiting with my parents a few days before, and we were told that the food was served on Christmas Eve at 5 p.m. My answer was; We eat anytime the food is served. The answer in return was; In Norway, we have a tradition to eat at 5 p.m, and that tradition is what we are continuing to do. No, I said, it is not written anywhere that it is a Norwegian tradition to eat at. 5 p.m. This tradition you guys have made up yourself. It is ok to eat at 5 p.m, let it be with that.

Faith moves mountains

In terms of faith, there is only one faith. The written Word of God and the commandments of God to you and me. There is only one truth, the only begotten Son of God - Jesus Christ. He who gave his life for all humanity crucified dead and resurrected again on the third day; Sits at the right hand of the Father. -Will come back to judge living and dead.

The Bible is given to us to know the truth and will of the Lord, and the Holy Ghost is given to us to be a powerful witness. As you stay close to the Lord, He will keep you close. When you read and meditate on His word day and night, you will start to know Him. It is only the Name of all names, Jesus Christ, God's only-begotten Son whom the Lord sent to the cross because He loved the world more than we ever can imagine.

If you stay close to the Lord and obey Him, you will grow up and become a giant in the Kingdom of God. As you obey the commandments and hate sin, you become the truth when you proclaim the truth to those who live in a world of lies. This world wants the truth, and they want the God of truth - Jesus Christ. They demand to be demonstrated that God exists, a God

who says, Come to Me, all you who labor and are heavy laden, and I will give you rest. (Matthew 11:28)
-When you decide to be the truth for those who carry heavy burdens.

Many preach about Jesus, but there are not many who preach the real Jesus.
Even Satan believes in Jesus and trembles.

Unbelief builds mountains - faith moves mountains

Faith moves mountains. But have you ever thought about what is involved in creating these mountains? Unbelief is one of the elements that you choose to allow into your life. As a result, you begin to build a mountain of disbelievers around you.
The Bible says; Go, lay your hands on the sick, and they will be healed. You do not want to believe, and this causes a mountain of disbelief to become the master of your life. Perhaps someone around you says you need the gift of healing to heal the sick. Well then, have you listened to an unbeliever. If you do not believe and act on it, your infidelity will build your mountain.
-This was just one example.

The Bible says

"Even so the tongue is a little member and boasts great things. See how great a forest a little fire kindles! And the tongue is a fire, a world of iniquity. The tongue is so set among our members that it defiles the whole body, and sets on fire the course of nature, and it is set on fire by hell." (James 3:5-6)

The Bible. The written Word of God to you and me. Believe, act on it, do not open the door for disbelief. Believe Jesus Christ, act as the **scriptures say**.

Listen;

"So Jesus answered and said to them, **have faith in God.** For assuredly, I say to you, whoever says to this mountain, Be removed and be cast into the sea, and does not doubt in his heart, but believes that those things he says will be done, **he will have whatever he says**." (Mark 11:22-23)

Notes;

_____

_____

_____

_____

_____

_____

_____

_____

CHAPTER 8

Finally

The final decision was taken, and the letter was sent. It is time for us to move on to the Lord's ministry. I now cancel our family membership in the church; ...Thank you for our time there, and we bless you all in the name of Jesus.

The Jailbreak was a fact. It was time for a new beginning.

Freedom
In the same way, as I received Jesus in the Vigeland's Park, in the same way, burdens were removed when the withdrawal was confirmed. Years of control were now broken. Why? Because when the announcement was a reality, I was no longer in agreement with the church's way of 'running' a church. The signature of our membership was now broken.
-It's only when you make choices with the Lord: you clearly understand that we do not wrestle against flesh and blood.

The powers and authorities have no authority before people accept their agenda
"For we do not wrestle against flesh and blood, but against principalities, against powers, against the rulers of the darkness of

this age, against spiritual hosts of wickedness in the heavenly places." (Ephesians 6:12)

If we are hanging out in a group that is not willing, it is a guarantee that not much will happen. All Christians must begin to understand that everything that is happening on this earth is of a spiritual matter. Then it's time to get into a spiritual understanding of what's going on around us in everyday life.
-It will only happen if you stick to God's written word, the Bible, and are trained by the Holy Spirit.

The Lord begins to show pictures of the Philippines
One day, God began to show me pictures from the Philippines. Not just once, but several times. Pictures were showing myself preaching the Gospel, healing the sick and casting out demons. All of this was in line with the Bible. There was no doubt this was from the Lord.

More pictures from the Lord to my wife and I
Time passed, and the Lord continued to show me the Philippines. But it was not yet the right time to go there. My wife had not received anything from the Lord that I had asked Him to do. But then came the day. Early one morning, I sat in the living room and read the Bible. My wife came running out of the bedroom and was completely overjoyed. She said; I dreamed of scripture in Luke's Gospel about healing the sick.
-Luke 10:8-9, I answered. Not long after, we were on our way to the Philippines.

Along the streets

It was a little quiet for the first few weeks in the Philippines.
Time went on, making banners for street evangelizing, as well as
some other preparations.

Healing

One of the pitfalls you get stuck in when you are in a church as a
newborn, is: few have faith in praying for the sick nor preach the
Gospel to the lost.

Most believe that one needs the gift to heal, or they do not think
they have anointing to accomplish it. Then Mark 16:18 becomes
something that you just 'pass' when you read the Bible and the
whole chapter becomes dead. There is not written much about
healing the sick, but what is written is for everyone and all.
It is a tragedy that the church has such a little understanding in
this area.

It's the first day in the Philippines with the new banner, and
down the main street, it went. On one side of the banner, it was
written; **Pain or any sickness, ask me for Healing**. On the other side; **Forgiveness is Wonderful**.

Later in that day, having trampled through almost the entire city,
I said to the Lord; Now I'm really on the school bench. I thank
you for having written in your word; We lay our hands on the
sick, and You heal. I had not come far down the street before
something happened.

In the middle of the door of a restaurant, there was a man with
big muscles. He looked skeptic on me and the banner.

I went straight to him and asked if he had any pain or illnesses in the body that he needed healing for. He had a shoulder that could not be lifted more than halfway up, something he had worn for several years. I asked if I could pray for him, and that he said 'yes' to. Right after I was finished praying, I asked; How does it feel now?

"A little better but not quite good," he responded.

- "Okay," I said and laid my hand on his shoulder and thanked the Lord for 100% healing. And there, the arm straightened up without any problems.

After this, it continued further down the streets where the next one was healed. For the rest of that month, I saw hundreds of people healed.

-If I can, then you can. Are you ready?

Liberation and Deliverance

Thousands of people saw the banner every single day. This made many to believe in what the banners said, and they came to me with their problems.

We must all be the light in a dark world. Is your light on so others who live in the dark can see Jesus through you?

"For so the Lord has commanded us: I have set you as a light to the gentiles that you should be for salvation to the ends of the earth." (Acts 13:47)

Healing's in numbers

In the first few weeks, I actively looked after sick to pray for. Many times, we were stopped on the streets of motorcycle taxis and cars, by people who had seen little hope in our banners.

People who had one or more family members in their homes
with hopeless diseases. We were driven both here and there to
pray for these poor people. People wanted prayer in the middle
of the street. Store owners came running after us and asked us to
come into their store and pray for their employees.

You may not think much about it, but if you get sick in this
country, you have to pay the entire hospital stay yourself. And it
is for sure not cheap either even you are in a country that most
things cost just a fraction of what it does in western countries.

I remember a lady that I encountered in a housing company. A
place that was nothing special if compared to the Western standard. Everything seems to be good with this lady, but suddenly
she opened up and started crying. She cried and cried. She tells
me she has lost feelings in large parts of all her fingers. She had
hard work in a kitchen, which she was utterly dependent on to
survive. If you get sick and are employed in the Philippines, it's
out the back door, and the company has hired a new one before
you're out of the building. Rights for workers do not exist much.
No governmental system that catches you up. You are left alone.

Now I stand in front of a mother with four children, and the man
left her a long time ago. She is alone.
You might think she's getting the children's contribution? It
does not exist in this country. It is quite clear that she can break
down at any time.
- "Can I pray for you?" I asked her.
She just sighed a weak yes.

-I grabbed her hands and talked life to them and gave thanks to the Lord for by His wounds: she has been healed.

(Isaiah 53:5 - 1 Peter 2:24)

Suddenly she lights up like a sun, moves her hands back and forth looks at them as if they are new.

-Healed.

The Bible says that the Lord is near the least. I have experienced this numerous times. I continue to preach to this lady, but it was hard cause she was utterly disturbed by the joy of what just happened.

Most Christians never come to experience this as I tell about here. Why not?

-Because they are not obedient to go out in the whole world with the Lord's powerful Gospel.

They are not available to those who need them.

This lady, who was healed from numbness in her fingers, was not only healed, but she got the spark back in her life. What was dead had has now become alive. At the end of our conversation, she says, "I have prayed for God to become healed so I can support my family. The day we met, that was the day the Lord answered her prayers. That day I was obedient to what the Lord has called me to do. That day, she received the answer to her prayer.

-Can you imagine the result if I was disobedient this day?

From row 13 to healing crusades

I sat at row 13 in the church and was not happy with my Christian life at all. I looked forward to every prayer day, every Sunday, and every gathering with other believers. Never did I found anyone with the same hunger for the Lord and His power. Many expressed their zeal to do mighty things for the Lord, but the fruit of their statements was not in line with what they spoke.

I always went home wondering what's going on. Were the Bible and God so intricate and advanced that it is not possible to come into what the Bible says?

-That's what happens when you're a bench slider along with a lot of other bench sliders.

Most think they are where they should be according to God's written words.

-What a big deception believers live in.

"They profess to know God, but in works they deny Him, being abominable, disobedient, and disqualified for every good work." (Titus 1:16)

It was after I decided to follow the mission commandment my Christian life began to become alive. He who sat on the 13-bench row set his place and travels to the other side of the earth. Held healing crusades, made disciples, cast out demons, and proclaimed and demonstrated the kingdom of God had come near.

-What a mighty God we have.

The true fellowship is how the Bible describes it, not how we feel it should be. Choose the right fellowship, or be drawn down to a level that chases on the experiences and feelings, and does not wholeheartedly seek Him who is the creator of the miracles.

84

Jesus wants us all to live a life in signs and wonders. A life in signs and wonders, to exalt His name, NOT OURS. His name, His miracles - through you.

The Holy Spirit is your helper to demonstrate the kingdom of God; To preach the Gospel to sinners to repentance.

It was time to do what a believer should do. Equip other Christians to do the job of preaching the Gospel, healing the sick, and casting out the demons. Yes, you read correctly. Many think it's the evangelist who is going to go out there and evangelize himself, but unfortunately, that is not true. All Christians have received the same commandment in Mark 16:15.

Listen;

The Lord gave some to apostles, some to prophets, some to evangelists, some to shepherds and teachers.

-Why?

For the Saints to be able to serve and to build the body of Christ. Why do we need it? So that we no longer be toddlers and let us throw and drift around the wind of each teaching by human play, by cleverly in the delusional trick of error.

Then it is not right that the pastor appears and is treated as the 'almighty' leader!

Today there is hardly an evangelist in what they call the churches. The 'leaders do not want them.'

Booy church

This church eventually became our collaborative partner when it came to food distribution at the local garbage filling, as well as different places around the poor areas of the city. The cooperation had lasted about one month when they were offered to be further equipped for the Lord's service. This they said yes to, and the following Sunday, we started.

It was how to preach the Gospel and heal the sick they should be trained in the first place. In short, all went on to believe God's written words, then act on it. After a few short hours in the classroom, we went out in the field and performed what they had learned. Everyone who was attending the first day prayed for several people who were healed.

Workers get training at work
Jesus trained His disciples out among people. I saw no reason to do anything else when this church was to be equipped. Jesus set the simplest standard, and we humans love to believe we have plenty of better solutions. Therefore, not very many Christians become particularly effective in their work for the Lord.

The disciples were with Jesus for about three years. At that time, they did not have the New Testament, nor were they born again and not baptized in the Holy Ghost. But they were willing to follow the Lord's commandments. A Christian today has the Bible, must be born again and baptized in the fire and power of the Holy Ghost. That is to say; We have gained full power to do the job. The Holy Spirit is ready 24/7, to teach you all things **when you go**.

The big conferences with all the 'anointed' ministers, they mean nothing if you are not willing to lay down your life for the Lord and begin to obey Him to go out to the unsaved and sick with the power and revelation of God. In this way, you are supposed to train other believers as well as reaching out your hands to the poor.

We met on the squares; Ekklésia
We go to churches. We are members of churches. We sit like candles in the churches. But do we know what the word congregation means?

From the basic text, the word Ekklésia "church" is defined as a congregation. It is from the word; Ek, which means; Out among. The word **Klesis**, which means a call. Ekklésia 'church' means to be **called out**.
-Who is calling us out? Jesus Christ.

Go into the <u>whole world</u> and preach the Gospel to every creature. (Mark 16:15)

Jesus calls us out, but we'll be seated. We sit and pray that the Lord will send people to 'our' church, into the building, until the altar for the altar call. But we are only open on Sundays. Otherwise, we are closed.
-This picture is seriously wrong.

Ekklésia began to take shape
It was Matthew 28:18-20 - Mark 16:15, which was written throughout the board in the small church in Tagbilaran City. Inside, many of the members had been sitting for a while. Seated and waited for something to happen. They had already been

taught how to pray for sick to be healed, and now it was time to take the next step.

We planned to meet on the squares the following Saturday. The Biblical Ekklésia should be gathered and demonstrate that the kingdom of God has come near. We were about ten people who went out to the squares.

Eight Saturdays, we were at eight different turfs. Those who had been sitting in the congregation and waited for something to happen prayed for 432 people who were healed from pain and illness during these eight days.

-This is what it's all about. To be where people are, reaching out our hands and proclaiming the wonderful Gospel of Jesus Christ.

Why are there so few coming to today's congregation?
Peter said to them, repent and be baptized. (Acts 2:38)
The Bible further states that people were daily added to the congregation. But it is not quite the same that is happening today. The message of repentance is something that is not preached as it should be done. This is one of the reasons why it is not like in the first church. Today, we believe we have it cause of great sermons. We want to do it differently than Jesus did, then the results will be wrong.

Luke 15
The Bible says; **All** the tax collectors and the sinners drew near to Him to Hear him. (Luke 15:1)

All tax collectors. All sinners

The sinners stayed close to Jesus: think about this. Where was Jesus when he preached? Out among the people. Then there is no reason we should not do the same. If Jesus did it this way, why do we think we have a better way to do it? Why can we not just do what the Lord has commanded us in the mission commandment? The Bible says; **Go!** The churches are sitting and waiting that the Lord will send the sinners through the door. If not the message of repentance proclaimed in the way it is supposed to be, Jesus would be excluded from the assembly. He may not be present as He wants to be present. Tragic but true. Everything else 'we believe' is more important than Jesus gave his life for, **the sinners**.

-The power comes from God's reviled word, nothing else. The true uncompromising God's written word. The message of repentance must be common in our preaching.

Who do you want to be?

One who talks about miracles or one who performs miracles? One who talks about the love of God, or one that embraces people and conveys God's love?

One who talks about everyone else who has a Ministry, or one who works in his ministry?

One who follows the 'pastor' in all that he says, or one who becomes what Jesus says through the Bible?

But why do you call me Lord, Lord, and not do the things which I say? (Luke 6:46)

Here all Christians must make a choice. Shall you obey or not?

CHAPTER 9

Koinonia - The fellowship

The life and growth of the Koinonia

"And they continued steadfastly in the apostle's doctrine and fellowship, in the breaking of bread, and in prayers. Then fear came upon every soul, and many wonders and signs were done through the apostles. Now all who believed were together, and had all things in common, and sold their possessions and goods, and divided them among all, as anyone had need."
(Acts 2:42-45)

Philippians 2:1-4 declares the following

"Therefore if there is any consolation in Christ, if any comfort of love, if any fellowship of **the Spirit**, if any affection and mercy, fulfill my joy by being like-minded, having the same love, being of one accord, of one mind. Let nothing be done through selfish ambition or conceit, but in lowliness of mind, let each esteem others better than himself. Let each of you look out not only for his interests but also for the interests of others."

Koinonia is to be consistent with each other; Are combined in purpose and serve side by side. Based on our shared koinonia with God, the Father, and His Son Jesus Christ. (1 John 1:3)

Can two walk together unless they agree? No

If the alleged fellowship does not have the same mind, it is not a fellowship, as the Bible shows us. But a fellowship based on a compromise on God's words and disorder. If you do not agree with the Lord and His commandments, but living life to pick out what suits you in scripture, you will never be able to have koinonia with others who have chosen the true biblical fellowship. What kind of fellowship is it when it's no order? And having the same mind, you cannot have with others before you agree with the Lord in one's life.

-It is not enough to say, but we are Christians, and then the scripture says we shall not stop meeting each other.

God will reveal His word to the one who is willing to Him.
-The Bible is God's Word and God Himself.

Church traditions of unwillingness are not something a believer should follow.

"If we say that we have fellowship with Him, and walk in darkness, we lie and do not practice the truth. But if we walk in the light as He is in the light, we have fellowship with one another, and the blood of Jesus Christ His Son cleanses us from all sin." (1 John 1:6-7)

The scriptures command us;

Honoring each other

"Be kindly affectionate to one another with brotherly love, in honor giving preference to one another." (Romans 12:10)

Live in harmony with one another
"Finally, all of you be of one mind, having compassion for one another; love as brothers, be tenderhearted, be courteous."
(1 Peter 3:8)

Accept each other
So it is in Christ Jesus I have my praise in God's service.
(Romans 15:17)

Serve one another in love
"For you, brethren, have been called to liberty; Only do not use liberty as an opportunity for the flesh, but through love serve one another." (Galatians 5:13)

Be kind and compassionate to one another
"And be kind to one another, tenderhearted, forgiving one another, even as God in Christ forgave you." (Ephesians 4:32)

The relationship between parents and children
"Let the word of Christ dwell in you richly in all wisdom, teaching and admonishing one another in psalms and hymns and spiritual songs, singing with grace in your hearts to the Lord."
(Colossians 3:16)

Encourage each other
"Therefore comfort each other and edify one another, just as you also are doing." (1 Thessalonians 5:11)

92

Motivate each other

"And let us consider one another in order to stir up love and good works." (Hebrews 10:24)

Offer hospitality to one another

"Be hospitable to one another without grumbling." (1 Peter 4:9)

Love one another

"Since you have purified your souls in obeying the truth through the Spirit in sincere love of the brethren, love one another fervently with a pure heart." (1 Peter 1:22)

This is easily told how a true Biblical koinonia should be amongst us.

Notes;

_____

_____

_____

_____

_____

_____

_____

CHAPTER 10

Be a doer of the Word
Not only a hearer

Be obedient to the word of God

To whom shall we be obedient? What does the scripture say about to whom you shall be obedient?

-Your feelings and voices you hear from internal and external influences?

If Jesus gives us a commandment to go out in the world, live daily in repentance and sanctification, and you either believe or act on this, have you then elevated yourself above the word of God? There was another who tried to build his kingdom, but he was thrown out of heaven forever. (Revelation 12:7-9)

Humility, the key to God's wisdom

God resists the proud but gives grace to the humble. (James 4:6)

Think about it. There is a very thin line between disobedience and obedience. But the outcome can be significant and painful. -It's all up to you.

Search yourself now. Be honest with what God has created. What you are now seeing in the mirror is yourself - the one whom the Lord has chosen to give the Holy Ghost.

A given Spirit from the Lord Himself right from the throne of heaven to you that you may work in signs and wonders, that men shall be saved and set free. Set free from demons, strongholds, and Satan's heavy yoke.

-It is you the Lord has chosen to bring His children back to Him. All the children of God that have gone astray. (1 Peter 2:25)

Do not deceive yourself

We are all called out in the whole world, but we are sitting at home and doing other things. If you do not believe in the written Word of God and His commandments, but you proclaim that you're a Christian, you have created yourself your own God, which is not anywhere else than in your mind.
Stop deceiving yourself and become a doer of the word. (James 1:22-23)

Look at the wonderful promise to you in James 1:25; "But he who looks into the perfect law of liberty and continues in it, and is not a forgetful hearer but a doer of the work, **this one will be blessed in what he does**."

Blessed in Greek is **Makarios**, it means; Supremely blessed when God extends His benefits.

Faith without action is dead

If you continue to deceive yourself, keep saying that you should not proclaim the gospel and heal the sick, we see in James 1:26 what the Lord says about you.

Verse 26;

"If anyone among you thinks he is religious, and does not bridle his tongue but deceives his own heart, this one's religion is useless."

On the way down

To walk with the Lord Jesus Christ is not as many believe or perhaps wish. It's about dying in yourself and fight the flesh until you sit on sore knees and wash the feet of others.

To be a disciple for others to get.
In today's church, it's the opposite; The church is built like a pyramid. You start at the bottom line and then work upwards towards the top. However, according to the Bible, it is seen that this is not the right way to do it. If you turn this pyramid upside down, it's easier to understand how the Lord wants it.

Listen;
"But he who is greatest among you shall be your servant."
(Matthew 23:11)

All believers shall live a holy life and not imitate the world

"And do not be conformed to this world, but be transformed by the renewing of your mind, that you may prove (discern) what is that good and acceptable and perfect will of God."
(Romans 12:2)

The Bible says

"Beware lest anyone cheat you through philosophy and empty deceit, according to the tradition of men, according to the basic

principles of the world, and not according to **Christ**."
(Colossians 2:8)

They called themselves leaders in the church we attend. For
these leaders, it was not appropriate to go out and preach the
gospel or pray for the sick on the street.
-This is not a leader at all.

If you take after this type of teaching, you will be taught to do
the same. Namely that everything should take place within the
church's four walls. Being an obedient Christian is hard work,
not to chase the last sermon, or follow others' goals and opinions.

We still hear about the ancient ministers
From the late 1800s until the mid-1970s. They performed miracles that hardly any Christians have heard of today. Go to You-
Tube and search for; A.A Allen, Jack Coe, T.L Osborne, you will
see the Holy Spirit move in a way that you do not see many
places today. At these meetings, thousands upon thousands were
met by the Lord. Many times we shout for revival, and we wonder why there is no revival today. It all looks dead.
-But what about today? Is not the Holy Spirit already here? Yes,
He is. Then there is only one thing that applies to you. You must
lay down your whole life, start walking with the Lord as He
says.

At A.A Allen's tent meet in the 50-60s, where people were rolled
inside the tent in wheelchairs, and themselves rolled out the
wheelchair. Parkinson's patients arrived laying in beds, and

walked out again themselves. Disabled people were rolled in lying in beds, and the crowd heard it clenched in the joints of him lying in bed when A.A Allen prayed for them. They were raised after years locked to a bed, secluded at the end of a corridor at an institution.

Looking at old pictures from the tent meetings to A.A Allen, it's not uncommon to see closest to the entrance to the tent; There were a lot of ambulances. The hospitals transported the ones with incurable diseases to A.A Allen's meetings.

-Is it any Christian who has faith in this today?

Hunger

Why is there so little 'action' today compared to in the old days? Where are the Crusades? Where is the healing?

Could not the 'popular' churches today agree with a recycling company for a metal container on the outside of the congregation? A container that was filled with crutches and wheelchairs during the last week of the Holy Spirit's led meetings? Unfortunately, this cannot happen before the church begins to obey God, as He says, not what the so-called pastor says. The latter is in the helping ministry, not in the lead role!

We, in the western part of the world, live in use and throw society, and most of us (think) we have what we need here in life. There is no urge among us. There is no urge in us crying for the Lord. Your neighbor may be in a wheelchair. He has all the help that he needs, and every day you see him with maybe with two assistants. He has a free taxi to get around. A huge team of people is there for his function, and you might think it's great that he gets all this help?

-Yes, of course, it is.

But the truth is, he is sitting in a wheelchair and is overrun by Satan. What he needs is the Lord. It's your hands and your prayers, all of you who are filled with the Holy Ghost.

Why do not you go out into the world of sins and reach out your hands? Because there is no longing in your heart to see the power of God change this world. We are too comfortable and busy with; Me, myself, and some more of myself. Most are satisfied with themselves and theirs.

-What a deceit we live in.

Think about this

If you make yourself available among people with a small sign that it says; Are you in any need of healing? What do you think will happen then? Well, the first thing to happen is that you will be bombarded with strange questions. But it's okay because you live a surrendered life to the Lord. If you do, Jesus promised that He is with those who obey. Then the most amazing will happen; Namely, people will be healed. If you obey, it is a written promise from He who has created the whole universe; If you lay your hands on the sick, He will heal.

- It's up to you now.

It works

If you do not have faith to pray for the blind, deaf, or cancer sick, start praying for people with pain. Do what you have faith for. Find someone with shoulder, knee, back, arm, or headache.

We see in Mark 16:18 (King James) that the word shall is used twice. The first time it is written as a commandment, the second time as part of a promise. You believe, as the Bible says in Matthew 17:20 and faith without action is dead. (James 2:26)

Then we act with faith in the commandment with a promise within. (Mark 16:18)
You believe the written word, lay your hands on someone who has pain, and commands it to go in the name of Jesus. Then people become healed, when you believe and act on the written word of God.

Faith with action is alive
When you decide to give to the needy, they will get it.

"He who believes in Me, **as the Scripture has said**, out of his **heart** will flow rivers of living water." (John 7:38)

Before, it will flow streams of living water out of you. Psalm 1:1-3 gives us a pointer on how close we must stay with the Lord in our daily lives.

"Blessed is the man who walks not in the counsel of the ungodly, nor stands in the path of sinners, nor sits in the seat of the scornful, But his delight is in the law of the Lord, and in His law, he meditates day and night. He shall be like a tree planted by the rivers of water, that brings forth its fruit in its season, whose leaf also shall not wither; and whatever he does shall prosper." (Psalm 1:1-3)

Become a Kingdom Demonstrator

Department Store, in a shopping center in the Philippines. After a long day in the street preaching the gospel of the Lord, purchasing of the daily needs was on the list of agenda. I needed some new towels, and on the top floor of the shopping center was a department store. Amid the shelves, there was a girl with a green uniform and hard makeup. As I approached her, the Lord began to show me things about her. When this happens, I've experienced that it's just opening your mouth and getting started. I went straight to her and did not waste any time. Pleasantly, I began to talk about the sin she had in her life and the direction it went. I hit the nail straight on the head. She burst out in a cry, and streams of tears ran down her cheeks. Then she says; How can you know all this? I pointed to Jesus and what the Bible says about sin and that repentance is required in her life. We still stand between red and black towels.

-The whole situation for her was now a little embarrassing. There she stands with a foreign man crying in the middle of a store. You have to be fast in such situations because you never know when a guard or the boss himself shows up.

Well, the message was delivered, and I continued to shop. Now it's up to her to take the next steps.

Today

You wake up and say to the Lord, 'Jesus use me today, send me on someone else's way.' Someone who needs a word of truth from you, Lord. If you speak this and believe it, the Lord will use you. But when you do this, do not be passive for it throughout the day. You must be willing and ready for the mission.

-We must think like we are born again.

When you grow

Then the demons get a problem. They cannot handle a Christian full of the Holy Ghost. But a lukewarm Christian is no match for either Satan or the demons. You will be laughed off. But if you live in the Lord, obeying the commandments of the Lord, grow up to man's maturity, Satan and the demons will have trouble. (James 4:7)

Diseases

There are many terrible diseases in the poorer parts of the world. Maybe you meet people with leprosy, skin diseases like lupus, diabetes that have eaten up large parts of the body. Lupus eats the skin and leaves large open holes in the body that does not grow.

Toothache is very common.
Many times you see people with egg-size toothaches. They sit there and hold their hands on the cheek. Many of them are just waiting for the pain to end. Most of them go through the day with a pain level that we can hardly imagine. Before the toothache is over, the next one is in progress.

In the West, we do not think much about diabetes. That's what the doctor takes care of. I have prayed for people in the Philippines who have diabetes with open wounds on large parts of the body that never grow. I especially remember a lady that I visited, when I entered her house, it was just like a wall of stench that hit me. It seemed as though I came to a slaughterhouse. The smell of open wounds lay like a thick blanket throughout the house. From the knee and down to the toes, it was only a big open wound. What might be the strongest she said was; I am waiting for amputation because no doctor can make me healthy, she said. Can you imagine it?

Sometimes they can afford medicines, sometimes not. Whole families go bankrupt because of this terrible disease. Doctors have tried all types of medication to get rid of diabetes.

The only chance they have to be healed is the power of the Lord through your hands. Your hands that obey Mark 16:18.

It's like learning to bicycle.

The first time it's a bit winding, but eventually, you're safer.

-That's how it is to pray for the sick.

In the streets as the Messenger of the Lord

When we have food distribution on the streets in the Philippines, there are always dozens of children of all ages coming. The parents of these children are usually not far away, and sometimes they also attend to have a small snack. When these parents see that you are one who prays for the sick, you will right away have a prayer line. What a blessing this is. When you agree with God's written word, you quickly find out that the devil is toothless. The roar will not scare you much.

The power of the Holy Spirit will work when you start using it.

The Bible says in Hebrews 4:2 - The word which they heard did not profit them, not being mixed with faith in those who heard it.

The Word of God, you take it and fill yourself by reading it. You already have faith. It is born into you in the new birth. But neither the Word of God nor your faith will be of any use to you if you do not act on it and use it. The word melts with the faith in your heart with faith in your spirit. The word faith is a verb, and all verbs are the words of action. See, for example, the verb; To walk. It helps nothing to stand on the street and shout; I go when you do not want to move your legs and do what you say. Then your confession will not matter to you. In the same way, it is with faith.

Use your faith in the Word of God by acting on it. Act as the word of God says.

Notes;

_____

_____

_____

_____

_____

_____

A doer gets revelations

A doer of the word
follow the Lord
and do not belong to pastors heard

When you seek you will find
otherwise, you will be blind

But if you search on the wrong ground
you will be lost and not found
down in the devils ground

Satan is wise
be not unwise
then you will not
get a hold of
the Lords advise

The lost matters

CHAPTER 11

What happens when you believe

We shall not convince people with great sermons and long preaching. The purpose of a Spiritful Christian Life is to demonstrate a living God who is above all things.

Example;
It is not written; If you want, you can lay your hands on the sick.
It is written; They will lay hands on the sick, and they will recover. (Mark 16:18)

You pray - it happens

Here are some testimonies of what I've experienced when I choose to believe and act on what the Bible says about going and proclaiming the gospel of the crucified Christ, laying hands on the sick and seeing them being healed.

The greatest thing is to be the love of Jesus, among the least.

I prayed

One day on the street, I preached to some taxi drivers, and at the same time, I asked them how the business was.
-Not particularly good, there are little passengers, that was the answer that I've got. Many times, taxi drivers complain whether

there are a lot or no customers at all. But I have passed the place where they have their regular route, and many times they are waiting for a long time for passengers. Those who drive fixed routes, they do not drive when they get a passenger, they have to wait until the taxi is full before the departure.

I asked one of them if I should ask the Lord to bless him financially? He would be more than happy if I would do that. I told him to lay his hands on mine, then I prayed and blessed him.
-A couple of weeks later, I met the same driver.
"Hello," I said, how has the last two weeks been?
He said, "I've never had so many passengers. Everything has just been amazing."
How was the second week? I asked him.
- "It was not that good," was the answer.
Okay, I said. What did you do with the Lord at this time? Did you take Him seriously?
-No, I did not, he said.
You see, Jesus He wants and be No.1 in your life. That's what He tries to tell you.

Mass raped
Bohol University. A considerable university, streets, and sidewalks full of people. My banner, thousands of people see in a place like this. On one side of the banner, it says; **Forgiveness is Wonderful**, with the following subtitle **Matthew 6:14**.
It was especially one guy I noticed. He stared hard at my banner. It was undeniable that he had reacted to what was written on it. He, I had to have a chat with. I swung right into the sidewalk and greeted this guy.

'How are you doing?' I asked.

It all proved to be a very special conversation lasting over half an hour. He said he was gay and that he has just returned from Saudi Arabia after a longer period with work.

He further explains that one night in Saudi Arabia. He had joined another man to his home for further "acquaintance." In the house, this man lived, 5-6 other men waited behind dark curtains. This was the start of a night of mass rape. 5-6 man who abused sexually this thin man who stood before me and opened up in detail of what had happened.

-Not that strange that my banner had gotten his attention.

Most of our conversation was about what sin is and how to repent of it and be set free. During the conversation, he suddenly looked deep into my eyes, and his own eyes were big like plates. Then it comes; I see Jesus in your eyes, that light it shines so strongly. I see the whole face of Jesus! Then it became silent. When the Holy Spirit works in this way, let Him have the time He wants.

It lasted a while, and then I proceeded to preach repentance and a relationship with our living God.

-That he saw Jesus in my eyes I have experienced before. It's just as exciting every single time. Never have I seen anything in these situations, but it is not necessary either.

This story probably would not have been possible without carrying a banner this day.

This man had, for a long time, carried this burden. No one had proclaimed repentance and forgiveness to him. But this day, that was the day he saw my banner. This day he had a meeting with the Lord our God. This day I was led to this area of the city.

-When you experience this, you understand the seriousness not to be obedient when the Lord wants something.

Healing testimonies.

The mango out sale

It was a mango fruit I wanted. The world's best fruit. Luckily the local fruit market was not far away from my house. The lady that worked there is approx. 60 years old.

-How are you? I asked her.

"Everything is ok," was the flat answer that I've got. This type of response often happens when you ask a stranger. When this happens, you have to change gear when it becomes how to use your God-given boldness. I went behind her little house and asked if she needed healing for anything.

-Yes, please, I've got pain in both my knees and that for many years. It was not hard to see because she almost cradled when she walked. I asked if I was allowed to come inside, so I should pray for her. There was a big smile on her, and she answered yes, so I went inside.

-I laid my hands on her knees and commanded all pain to go in the name of Jesus. Her smile was just getting bigger, and then it came; It's gone, the pain is gone! It was time to share the gospel of our Lord and Savior.

-I left with the mango and a great watermelon as a bonus. Glory.

The guard at the mall

It was just before closing time at the shopping center. We were
on our way home, my son and I, after some small purchases. In
the Philippines, there are always armed guards at the entrance of
the malls. Entrance's input is well-covered by shotguns and ba-
tons. As we approached the exit, I see the one guard holding a
Remington 700 pump shotgun in one hand and a big ice bag in
the other. The ice bag he pushed into his jaw: it was not difficult
to understand that this guard had a toothache. In this country,
there is no such thing as sick leave for the employees. If you are
not at work, there will be no payment. Therefore, you often see
people struggling through everyday life for daily bread. We
stopped by the guard and asked if he had a toothache.
-He just nodded weakly and was almost blurred in his eyes.
I asked my son if we should pray for him. "Yes, daddy" was the
answer.
-I laid my hand on his jaw and commanded all pain to go in the
name of Jesus. How do you feel now? I asked immediately after
I prayed.
-Better, he answered.
I thanked the Father for by His stripes: this guard has been
healed. Now the guard takes the ice bag away from his cheek,
looks strange at it, and looks odd at me. Suddenly he threw the
ice bag in the garbage box that stands right at the door.
-Healed.
We gave thanks to Jesus for everything, and I could go home
and put the little boy in bed.

11-year-old boy with arthritis

We had been out most of the day with our banners and evange-
lized. We were on our way home, and a couple of hundred feet
from where we had parked the car, three women sat on the road-
side and sold grilled bananas. We were tired after miles of walking, and I was tempted not to stop witnessing them. Every time
that thought comes, it's just obeying the scripture and not your
feelings. We stopped and asked if any of them had any pain or
illnesses they needed healing for.

-They were healthy all three, but then one of the ladies says;
Someone is living behind the house here that has arthritis. Perhaps you can go there and ask?

-Thanks, I said, and we went to the back of the house. In the
backside, it was probably 8-10 people that relaxed in a small
sofa group made of bamboo.

- "Hi" I greeted, is it someone here who has pain or illnesses
they need to be healed from? Then a man approx. 40 years old
arise. You could see that he had pain in one leg. It was arthritis.

-One in the team began to tell this man about Jesus while I
spoke to his wife. During the conversation, the man is healed
from arthritis, and he jumped around with the world's biggest
smile. Then the woman tells me; I have an 11-year-old who has
arthritis.

-What? I answered!

"Yes," she said, and there he is.

I turned around, and there was a boy who could barely walk
even he used a cane. It was not difficult to see that he was in terrible pain. I went straight to him and said, "Hi my name is Rune,
and now I'll pray for you." I laid my hand on his knee and

commanded arthritis to leave in the name of Jesus. Immediately after I said, "You don't need that cane anymore, start walking."
It was a brave boy who took the first steps without the cane.
- "How does it feels like?" I asked him.
"It is better," answered a skeptical little boy.
I thanked the Lord for by His stripes: this boy had been healed.
Then I said to the boy, Run!
Then he looked very strange to me. Come on, I said, and he took off like a rocket.
-Healed.
The next ten minutes, my friend and the boy had several running competitions around on the plot there.
-I just stood there and watched joyfully.
The day we showed up that day, the boy and his father were healed for arthritis.

What they did not tell me until after, was the day we arrived, the boy had been carried home from school by his classmates. This is because he had so much pain in one leg that he could not walk any further. Imagine a future life that this boy had.
-But Jesus Christ, our mighty Savior, had other plans.
A little further down the same street, we run a food distribution project, and this boy participated for several months after he had been healed. Basketball, that's his thing.
-What a mighty God we have.

Sore feet
I had been called to a place to pray for someone with pain. It was a place where most people had a hard time to get funds to

the daily bread. The man in the house came home from work, and he did not have a good day.

-What's wrong? I asked him.

"My feet," he said, they are almost killing me. They are so tender and sensitive under the fact that I can no longer go without shoes. Just inside on flat surfaces, I can walk without shoes.

-We must pray to the Lord, I told him.

It was okay, and I started praying. What's exciting about praying for the sick and afflicted is that after you've asked them how they are, most of them are fearless to find out if they're healed or not. The same thing happened this time, off with the shoes and out on the gravel it went. A little bit gentle in the beginning, then he disappeared down the road.

-Healed.

The driver with numb hands

There is one thing that Philippine people certainly do not like, and it's rainy weather. One day, we had 13 teenagers out with us in the streets. This day, it rained like never before. There we stood well under a roof, and on the other side of the road, there was a long line of taxi motorcycles.

-I looked over at them, and one of them got my attention. If it's raining a bit, it's not that important for me and over the road I went.

-How are you? I asked him.

Immediately he began to rub his hands. Not good was the answer.

-What's wrong?

My hands are numb. And I drive 12 hours every single day, he says.

It was raining hard now, and the preaching he received was not very long. I told him to lay his hands on mine; Then I commanded the numbness to go in the name of Jesus.

-How are your hands now?

He rubbed and rubbed his hands, better and better they became, and the smile grew bigger and bigger.

-Healed.

Healing line inside a Catholic church

Amid all the houses in the small district of Gasanai, there is a small Catholic church. We have some friends who live right next to that church, and one day I was out evangelizing, I went there for a visit. We sat outside and had a friendly conversation, and there is no way to avoid to look inside this little church. Kneeling pads on the benches, statues of Virgin Mary, Santo Nino, etc. This religion is about one thing, and it is to pray for idols.

Jesus is just an offspring from Mary, whom they think is God's mother.

But this day, the Lord opened a door for me to serve these people in the little church. Not from the pulpit but in the aisle of the church just before the mass began.

-I decided to go straight into the church and grab the first person standing there. It was an older lady who was one of the leaders there.

-I asked her; Is there someone here who needs healing from any pain or illness?

Yes, I need it. the lady said, my back has been hurt for a long time.

-Okay, can I lay my hands on your back and pray to Jesus, I said?

She agreed, and I had barely started to pray before her face started to smile. Healed.

Now it started to come more people to the church. Suddenly the old lady began to share with the others about her healing. Then the impossible happened; I now have a prayer line in the aisle of the church. People stood in a row in the aisle, and they were all healed from various ailments.

One of the ladies, she even called me Jesus. That was the first time someone said to me.

Outside the church, I continued to preach to an 80+-year-old woman. In the middle of the conversation, she says; I had to come home to her house because her daughter in law had a disease that the doctors did not manage to diagnose. She further said that she had a fever every single day, and I was very welcome to come as quickly as possible.

-I'm coming tomorrow was my answer.

The next day as agreed, I sat with the daughter-in-law and shared the gospel. She had been a believer throughout her life, but the faith of a Catholic in the Philippines is not built on God's written words. Nor do they have a personal relationship with the Lord. It is based on Ecclesiastical traditions and Ave Maria's prayers. When you preach to these people, it does not matter if they have been believers for a whole life. If they do not know God's written words, the Bible must be opened, and the basics must be presented. Just over an hour, we kept on reading different things from the Bible. After this, she got a prayer, and the Lord appeared with His incredible presence as He only can do. After this, I challenged her to go down with me to the Catholic Church, and I would show her a little about what we just read about in the Bible.

And she would love to.

-We stood outside her church and looked in. In the Philippines, it is hot all year long, and they usually do not have windows in the churches. I opened the word of God and shared from Exodus 20:4-5 and Colossians 2:8. I showed her the scriptures and challenged her to read them aloud.

-She did, and I told her to read the scriptures several times. Suddenly during the reading, she stops and lift her one hand and place it in front of her mouth, I never thought of what is written here she says!

-Here we see in simplicity that people believe, but they will not enter the true faith if it has no foundation in God's written words.

"And you shall know the truth, and the truth shall make you free." (John 8:32)

We went back to the house and continued where we left. A couple of older ladies came to visit, and before they had settled down, they were asked if they had any pain or illnesses they needed healing for.

-They both had.

I told the girl that it was her who would pray for these two ladies, and when she did, they would be healed.

I'm not ready for it, she replied.

-You are ready, I said. Come here, I'll show you.

The one lady had problems in the right hip region but had not been examined with the doctor to find out why. She also had pain every single day.

-Okay, now we have located the pain, now you lay your hand on her hip and command it to be healed in the name of Jesus. Okay? I told her.

Okay, she said and did it. She prayed a long prayer, not a short one that she was told to do. But it's not always easy to do everything right the first time.

-Done, she said and looked strange at me.

Ask the lady how she feels. I instructed her.

She did, and the older lady said she felt warm from her hands when she prayed for her. She was told to get up and go for a walk. All the pain is gone she said and smiled like a sun.

-There's one more lady, I told her. Now, you go to her and ask the same way as the previous one. If she has any pain or any illness, lay your hands on her and pray in the same way.

-It turned out that she had heart problems of unknown character, and back pain in the upper back. She laid her hands on her and prayed. The presence of God came so strong that we had to wait a couple of minutes to talk to this lady.

-Minutes went before she got the question: how do you feel? She felt peace, and the pressure in the breast region was gone.

This day the Lord used a Catholic woman to pray for two other Catholic women, to show that He is the Lord our Healer.

-Not only the healer but His willingness to heal sinners.

Half the face numb

A family of four lived on the street under a shed. These we got the opportunity to help by hiring a little flat to them through some acquaintances. One day I was down there to see that everything was okay. While the house owner and I sat in the backyard, a friend of her came. She was distraught and inter-rupted us. They only spoke their local language, and I do not understand that much. But there was one thing that was repeated several times in a few minutes, and that was; Trust Jesus, trust Jesus.

-Now I had to break in and hear what's going on. She began to tell me that she had no feeling in her upper lip and half the left side of the face. She was very disturbed and stammered that she was terrified to die.

-I told her Jesus is our healer. And if you want, I can pray for you. She was so happy to hear that so she said yes before I was finished talking.

-I laid my hands on her face and commanded the numbness to go in the name of Jesus. Then I gave thanks to the Lord for the healing.

-How do you feel now?

She smiled like a sun from one ear to the other. Then she starts hugging me as if we had known each other for years.

-This lady met me this day. She came with the fear of death, re-turned home healed and joyful. Thank you very much, Jesus.

Healing on our way home from the garbage disposal

Right next to the garbage pile where we had the food distribu-tion, there is a small factory that produces cement blocks. We had just wrapped it for the day and were on our way home.

There was full activity at the factory when we passed it, but it was something that I reacted to when I looked into the factory area. There was a man on the ground, that got a massage by another man. This seemed a little strange, so I swung into the area to ask what was going on. I shouted out of the car window to them if everything was as it should?

-Everything was alright, was the answer I got back.

I was not satisfied with his answer, so I turned off the engine and went to them.

-What is wrong with you since you lay on the ground? I asked. Only the muscles are tired after a hard day of work, was the answer.

-I was also uncomfortable with this answer, so I asked where else did he have pain?

In my chest, he said.

It was not hard to see that this guy had been out on a stormy day before. For six or seven places on his body, there were big scars after knife stabs. The next question was then simple; Did you get the chest pain after you got stabbed?

Yes, he said.

Can I pray for you? I asked him.

Yes, was the answer.

About 10 seconds into the prayer, he begins to smile, not just a little but a lot.

-Do you feel something? I asked him in the middle of the prayer. The pain is leaving, he said with a smile that grew bigger and bigger. Then suddenly, he began to breathe like a racehorse and was now completely confused that he could breathe normally again. Healed.

-What a mighty God we have.

EJL Commercial Store

One day I walked in the middle of the street with my banner: it came a man from behind and stuck on my shoulder. Do you have time to join me a little bit? He said. Sure, I said and followed him.

-Inside a store, we went, and the banner I parked on the outside. At the end of this crowded store, a lady was working.

-Hello, I said, what can I do for you here today?

She was a bit shy this lady, but eventually, she loosened up.

-I have a brother that is on drugs, she said. And I wonder if you can pray for him?

-Where is he? I answered.

He is not here, and he is in our house.

This was strange, and there must be something else to do here than just praying for one who is not even present. Okay, I will pray for him, but how are you? I asked the lady.

Then it came, she had pain several places in her body. But I felt it was more than just that.

-I asked if she had some unsettled things with someone, like unforgiveness and misunderstanding? Before she was able to answer, she got to know what the Bible says about the topic.

-Then the tears came, flowing down her cheek. She cried and cried so hard that she almost fell off the chair that she was sitting in.

There was a little doubt what was the problem.

-Now I told her, it does not matter what you feel, but now you start to forgive and do it loudly so I can hear it.

She began to forgive.

It took some time, but eventually, the breakthrough came.

"You can believe the others who both worked and traded in the store had big eyes, but they said nothing.

-Now it was time to pray for the plagues she had.

I prayed, and the Lord healed.

This lady was now thoroughly disturbed and started to tell the others in the store what just happened. She was so filled with joy about everything she had experienced in the last half hour. It was now time to pray for the others in the store, and several were healed for various pain.

I left the store, raised my banner, and continued down the street.

I cannot eat food because it hurts so badly when I swallow
There was conference time in Canhayupon in the Philippines, and I was one of those who would preach. After I finished it, I sat outside the entrance and talked to some friends. It was a full house, and people were everywhere. I started to get hungry while I was sitting there. Suddenly there's a 6-7 years old girl that approaches me.

Hi, can you help me? She said.

-Sure, what do you need help for?

My throat is so painful, and I do not manage to swallow when I eat. And now, I'm very hungry. The little girl said with a very sad face.

-When you are around, preaching the gospel, sick children are something that you will encounter. It's very tough at times to see all the little kids that are struggling with different kinds of is-sues.

-Shall we pray to Jesus, or what do you think?

We can pray to Jesus, the little girl said with a small voice.

-I prayed and gave thanks to the Lord for the healing.

-How are you now? I asked when I was finished praying.

Now, I am much better, she answered.

Children do not always express themselves much. This is where your humility will pave the way for what is needed to be done.

-I said, let's go to the back of the church where the big kitchen is. In the kitchen, it was more than ten people busy cooking. I asked one of the chefs there if it was possible to get two huge meals.

-We got it, and the little girl ate and ate. Healed.

-I sat next to her but did not eat much. I greatly appreciated what the Lord had done.

After the meal, I went back and sat in the same place again. Ten minutes later, a woman came with her little daughter in her arms because she had a high fever.

-The Lord healed, and the girl was up and running again. Glory.

Around 11 pm., I was in the kitchen again to take a look. In the midst of all that happened there, it appeared 5-6 big men who wanted a healing prayer. They had not attended the conference, and on their way to the kitchen, they passed a 60-70 other Christians. Why they came to the kitchen to me, it's only the Lord who knows.

They were now standing in line for prayer. I prayed, and the Lord healed. A lady was baptized in the Holy Spirit, and the rest was healed from a lot of different problems.

-This was my kitchen ministry for this time.

"Jesus Christ is the same yesterday, today, and forever."
(Hebrews 13:8)

122

Notes;

_____

_____

_____

_____

_____

_____

_____

_____

_____

_____

_____

_____

CHAPTER 12

On the frontline

Philippines

Months with preaching the gospel, healing the sick and casting out demons. Equipping the saints and massive attack from the enemy was on the daily agenda.

-The victory was there from day one.

People were healed in multitudes, set free from the demons, and the Philippine people saw Jesus Christ in action. It is us, Christians that shall perform this. Anointing oil, banners, tracts, healing cloths are part of the tools one can use to get the job done. A willing and obedient heart is what you need, but it helps with some additional equipment.

Where shall the job be done?

Is it just in your backyard you shall evangelize? Or has the Lord said; Go ye into all the world? (Mark 16:15)

What do you believe in? Where is your action directed? Have you listened to all the 'spiritual matured' brothers and sisters in the Lord around you? Or has it crept in total confusion when it comes to the simple written word of God?

The Bible says; **Go** into all the world and preach the gospel to every creature.

-It cannot be easier than this.

It is only the written word of God in the Bible we should relate to, nothing else.

You may say, "I do not have a call to go into the entire world and preach the gospel."

-The country you are living in is a part of the whole world.

How do we perform the job?

To prepare to preach the gospel is to say you are not living in it. When Jesus talks about a relationship in the Bible, He talks about an eternal relationship. A relationship that starts here on earth and will never end. People live so far away from the Lord, that it is almost embarrassing to call himself a believer. You just have to decide, who is your Lord, Jesus Christ, or; I will not? If you go, you have the world's best and most powerful helper on your right side - The Holy Spirit.

What is needed to perform the job?

Faith, will, reading, and acting on God's written word.

Tools for the job.

Banners

The first time I saw one carrying a banner with an evangelical message on, it was in the country of Norway. Immediately when I saw the banner, I knew this was something for me. It was simply amazing to see the attractive banner with the word of God written all over it. What a powerful tool for evangelism.

Nothing I knew about banners, but to get hold of one was necessary. The next week I sat a lot on the web searching. I found several different banners, but I did not find out about how to get hold of one. Something was wrong. The enemy was not particularly interested in that I should be a banner carrier. Months passed by, and I still had no banner. Besides, the Lord had begun to give me visions about the Philippines.

A day in life

We decided to go to the island of Bohol. Upon arrival, I started to make my own banners. From the first day, I began searching for materials. It was a success. One thing after another just fell into place, and not long afterward was the first banner set finished.

It was time for testing

Down the main street, it went, and thousands of people saw God's message up close that day. A banner is a powerful tool to reach out with. Many banners were produced, which was used in training other believers.

A banner simplifies the way to get in touch with people. If you find it difficult to reach out, a banner is something to consider. You walk down the street, and people see the banner at a distance, then it is much easier to start a conversation.

Tracts

How many times have you been rejected when you're going to tell people about Jesus? This is due to several reasons, and the enemy has a hand in the game here. People on the move, they are busy with themselves and their own. Perhaps they are standing and chatting in a corner, where you come and want to preach about Jesus. They are, of course, not interested in anything else than what they are talking about. To get in between in such situations is not always easy, and many times you will be rejected. This is where a tract does its job. One just sneaks a tract between them, and in most times, they take it. If they do, the door is open so you can boldly start to share the gospel.

Handkerchiefs and aprons

"Now God worked unusual miracles by the hands of Paul so that even handkerchiefs or aprons were brought from his body to the sick, and the diseases left them and the evil spirits went out of them." (Acts 19:11-12)

The first time I read this passage, I thought, "if Paul can, then I can."

This was something that we had to try out. We went to the mall, and several square meters of fabric was purchased. At home, I laid my hands on the material and prayed in Jesus' name. It was extraordinary; It felt as if a fire came out of my hands.

We cut the fabric up into small strips, put it in a small plastic pouch, with a little homemade 'how' to use patch inside.

Many of the people you meet in a city often live in rural areas. Often they have family members sick at home, and an apron cloth is a blessing to bring home.

-There is no shortage of Lord's promises of healing when you choose to believe and act on it.

Bibles

God's written word is what I taught. Why not show it to the people, just like the banners? A small Bible that can fit in a fanny pack, and that is what I have with me out. Besides, I have made white stickers covering the entire Bible on both sides. On the one side, it says, Holy, and on the other side; Bible.

T-shirts

If banners are inadequate or there is too little space to utilize them, jackets and T-shirts with a similar message on is very efficiently. Several times we had prayer lines inside stores. If you have a t-shirt with a gospel message on, there will be no question about who is doing what.

In most cities, you will find stores that print and design T-shirts. One of the times we made some, the owner of the store had terrible neck pain. While the t-shirts were in print, the owner experienced the Lord's healing power and was healed.

Boldness

Maybe you think that you are not particularly bold. But the Lord has promised in His written word, that if you use your boldness, the reward is great.

We are not talking about if you have boldness or not, but it is your will that implements the boldness.
-Do it - Grow in it.

"And he went into the synagogue and spoke boldly for three months, reasoning and persuading concerning the things of the kingdom of God." (Acts 19:8)

"In whom he have boldness and access with confidence through faith in Him." (Ephesians 3:12)

"Therefore do not cast away your confidence, which has great reward." (Hebrews 10:35)

The key
The power comes from the revelation of God's written word. When you believe and act on what the Bible says, it will function. Preach about repentance, Jesus crucified dead and risen, and the Lord will manifest His written word with signs wonders and miracles. Empty convictions of preaching to people are not what a Spirit-filled Christian shall do. He shall demonstrate the kingdom of God with the power of the Spirit. Neither more or less.

"For God so loved the world that He gave His only begotten Son, that whoever believes in Him should not perish but have everlasting life." (John 3:16)

We shall call sinners to repentance
Jesus came for no other reason than for sinners. Likewise, we
shall preach to the lost.

"I have not come to call the righteous, but sinners, to repentance." (Luke 5:32)

"From that time Jesus began to preach and to say, Repent, for
the kingdom of heaven is at hand." (Matthew 4:17)

We have all been assigned a size faith
No matter what kind of people you meet, if they are atheists,
Muslims, punks, gays, never forget that the Lord has imposed all
humans eternity. If you then preach the true gospel, there's
enough truth in all people to grab it.

Eternity has He imposed our hearts. (Ecclesiastes 3:11)

Without holiness, no man shall see the Lord
"Pursue peace with all people, and holiness, without which no
one will see the Lord." (Hebrews 12:14)

Sanctification is a word of truth many have read, but few think
of it. Most of the time, people forget, for without holiness, no
man shall see the Lord.
Often it is Ephesians 6:12-18 that is preached; For we do not
wrestle against flesh and blood, but against principalities and
powers, etc. But the important thing here is overlooked most of
the time is verses 1-9, namely, about sanctification.

"Blessed are the pure in heart, for they shall see God."
(Matthew 5:8)

"Flee also youthful lusts; but pursue righteousness, faith, love, peace with those who call on the Lord out of a pure heart."
(2 Timothy 2:22)

God's word the Bible
Read it, act on it, hesitate no longer.

The prodigal world
This world is doomed. We live in a materialistic time, where usage and disposal are what matters. People are looking for a Savior, but do not know where or how to look. Others say they have everything they need, and Jesus is then not necessary. Many have problems to close the garage door, cause of everything that floats over inside. No God, they 'think' they need.

Where are the rescue workers?
-The Lord is not particularly impressed by the congregation when He says; The harvest truly is plentiful, but the laborers are few. (Matthew 9:37)

The Bible says you cannot serve two masters
When it comes to money, it is not they who are the problem. But the love of those makes them the Lord in your life.
(Matthew 6:24)

In most cities in the U.S.A., many stores are open 24/7. There is no question about if this world is running in high gear. People are looking feverishly everywhere to find their inner selves. The Lord says that the only way to Him is through His Son Jesus Christ. It is an extremely urgent need for spiritually mature Christians to act powerfully to the lost in a lost world.

-I am the way, the truth, and the life. No one comes to the Father except through Me. (John 14:6)

"And this gospel of the kingdom will be preached in all the world as a witness to all the nations, and then the end will come." (Matthew 24:14)

The Lord wants all people to be saved
-God, our Savior, who desires all men to be saved, and to come to the knowledge of the truth. (1 Timothy 2:4)

There is victory in Jesus' name
"Having disarmed principalities and powers, He made a public spectacle of them, triumphing over them in it."
(Colossians 2:15)

Satan shoots arrows and will try to destroy everything that you do.
Your relationship with the Lord, friends, family, indeed, is all that you engage in. There are no limits on what Satan wants to try on, but fortunately, there is a solution; **God, His written word the Bible, well-knit with the Holy Spirit**.

Your thought life, the place where Satan is working hardest.

Think about this; You may not have been saved before you are midlife, then you have in your whole life lived together with your thought life. You have become accustomed to your thoughts. But then you got saved. The Holy Spirit dwells in you, and things begin to happen. Before you were saved, you were no threat to Satan. But when the Spirit of revelation dwells in you, then it all becomes completely different. You have now become a threat to Satan and all the demons.

-Now they will do everything they can to get the better of you and destroy everything that you do. Take the life of you and your entire family are on Satan's daily agenda.

"The thief does not come except to steal, and to kill, and to destroy. I have come that they may have life and that they may have it more abundantly." (John 10:10)

We read in Ephesians 6:16 that the devil shoots fiery darts (thoughts to your mind) at you. It says in the same chapter how to resist these arrows.

The Bible says in Matthew 6:6;
"But you, when you pray, go into your room, and when you have shut your door, pray to your Father who is in the secret place; and your Father who sees in secret will reward you openly."

Prayer closet means; Piece in a small room inside the human being. If you have trouble finding tranquillity, make a place for this now on the daily agenda.

-This is not soaking or meditation. Here we are going into the Lord's presence in the sharpened state. Now you are in a training camp with the Lord, and Satan hates that you shall have any breakthrough here.

You sit there and talk a little with the Lord, and when you are finished talking, it's time for listening. While listening, there comes surging a lot of thoughts. All these you need to train to take captive to the obedience of Christ. (2 Corinthians 10:5)

Not a single thought you shall 'just' accept.
It is in the silence you become sensitive to discern between Satan and God. This is where the Lord will train you in how to distinguish between the voices in your mind. It may take time to come through here, but by all means, never give up.

"Draw near to God and He will draw near to you. Cleanse your hands, you sinners; and purify your hearts, you double-minded." (James 4:8)

The Bible says you shall meditate on it day and night.

We must be rooted in the word as we learn to withstand the fiery arrows that are shot against us.

A challenge for you
Many countries in the world are currently in total distress. There are many sick and frail, yes you can hardly count them. Most of these people live in places where hospitals are privatized. This means that most of them cannot afford to seek out those when

they need it. There are public hospitals, but also they are not free. When people in the western part of the world have a toothache, we go to the dentist. In poor countries, they are sitting at home until it all aches out.

If you travel to a place like this and reach out your hands, then you are the love of Jesus among the smallest. The ticket can be found online, and to India will cost you around 500 USD.

"Let your conduct be without covetousness; be content with such things as you have. For He Himself has said, I will never leave you nor forsake you." (Hebrews 13:5)

These signs shall follow those who believe
They will lay hands on the sick, and they will recover.

This world demands to meet God's anointed that comes with the power of God and the true gospel.

The world wants it - You have it
Miracles will happen when you start to give out of what you've got, why?
-Because God's word says it, just believe it. **Do it**.

Notes;

_____

_____

_____

CHAPTER 13

In today's 'churches'

Many today have an attitude that suggests something like this; Believers must 'come' to an agreement so we can build the Kingdom of God. It may well not be so hard to be agreed in Christ?
-Here we see two attitudes that apparently 'feels' right, but has no coverage in God's written word.

One day I received an email.
It contained a link to a video on YouTube, as referred to Mr. Copeland and his entourage. They were, of course, broadcasting live on TV, and this day they had celebrated visitor from several places around the world. Many 'christians' on Facebook were involved in this video, and most of them agreed on one thing; Now, we all must agree in the faith.
It didn't matter what faith you had because we have the 'same' God.

How can someone that proclaims to be a born again Christian say something like that?
-One thing is to say you are born again; Another thing is to be born again and live like one.

The first thing that strikes me is; Have they ever read the Bible?
Yes, I believe so. Did they understand what they read? No, I do
not think so.

Lord means; Supreme authority - He who decides.
-If you pronounce that Jesus Christ is your Lord, why is He not
then Lord of all the areas in your life?

The Bible warns us against false Christians
In this context, it seems that repentance is excluded from most
teachings and preaching. God Yahweh, in its grandeur and simplicity, has given us His commandments through Scripture. You
will not find in Scripture where you shall go in agreement with a
sinner, but you will find the opposite.

The Bible says
"Do not be unequally yoked together with **unbelievers**. For
what fellowship has righteousness with lawlessness? And what
communion has light with darkness?" (2 Corinthians 6:14)

Unbelievers; Greek; Apistos; **One who does not believe**.

Infidel. Infidel is a derogatory term used when someone does
not believe the central principles of one's religion.
-Unbelievers in this context mean in all simplicity; **Disobedience to God**.

All believers must walk in unity with Jesus Christ and His written Word, no one else. Are you a born-again Christian, then you
have gone in agreement with the Lord and His written Word.

The old you have repented from sin then started to follow the Lord. No other than the Lord shall we go in agreement with. Many say they follow Jesus, but the evidence that you are born again and live like one, is that you do what Christ says.

Let us read about the Pharisees and the Sadducees leaven
We read in from Matthew 16, verse 6; "Then Jesus said to them: Take heed and beware of the leaven of the Pharisees and the Sadducees."
And verse 12; "Then they understood that He did not tell them to beware of the leaven of bread, but of the **doctrine** of the Pharisees and the Sadducees."

A religious community that has leaven in their learning. Time passes, and all that takes after their acceptance with their teaching becomes permeated with its leaven.

When one speaks the truth, one speaks the truth
But if one speaks contains little leaven, the whole dough is sour. -Let me explain it simply; Is it a little untruth or falsehood, it is all a lie.

The sourdough is in the Scripture used as an image of impurity malice and hypocrisy.

It is of great importance that all who believe develop his belief after God's word.

"But the Helper, the Holy Spirit, whom the Father will send in My name, He will teach you all things, and bring to your remembrance all things that I said to you." (John 14:26)

"Till we all come to the unity of the faith and of the knowledge of the Son of God, to a perfect man, to the measure of the stature of the fullness of Christ." (Ephesians 4:13)

Why should we get into a perfect man in Christ?

"That we should no longer be children, tossed to and fro and carried about with every wind of doctrine, by the trickery of men, in the cunning craftiness of deceitful plotting." (Ephesians 4:14)

The Bible says
"For there is one God and **one** Mediator between God and men, **the Man Christ Jesus**." (1 Timothy 2:5)

God Yahweh has given humanity the true Bible with its 66 books.

Warning against teaching that there is no coverage for in the word of God
"For I testify to everyone who hears the words of the prophecy of this book; If anyone adds to these things, God will add to him the plagues that are written in this book: and if anyone takes away from the words of the book of this prophecy, God shall take away his part from the Book of life, from the holy city, and

from the things which are written in this book."
(Revelation 22:18-19)

Philippines

One time we had campaigned in rural areas in the Philippines, I
met some elderly ladies. They had lived in the village for many
years. I asked a simple question. "You've gone to the Catholic
Church more or less every Sunday, right?"
"Yes," they replied, "in the last 40 years."
What is it primarily you remember the priest taught you about in
the church?
-They said, "He talked over the years that he was a messenger
from God, and we did not have to do anything else than to listen
to him. For it was he who was the scholar, and if you are not a
scholar, then you will be blind on your journey, and would then
not understand what is going on. Nor will you not understand
where to go, what kind of church you shall go to, or where to
give your tithing and reap what you sow. For the Bible, it was
only for specially selected by God, who could understand. We
just needed to go to church every Sunday, giving our donations,
and listen to the pastor's message from God.

The Bible gives us the answer

"This book of the law (the Bible) shall not depart from your
mouth, but you shall meditate on it day and night, that you may
observe to do according to all that is written in it. For then you
will make your way prosperous, and then you will have good
success." (Joshua 1:8)

Idols

What is an idol, and what does the Lord say about this?

An image

"You shall make no molded gods for yourselves."
(Exodus 34:17)

Put to shame all they that serve graven images. (Psalm 97:7)

They changed the truth of God into a lie and worshiped and served the creature more than the Creator. (Romans 1:25)

Strange gods

"And Jacob said to his household and to all who were with him, put away the foreign gods that are among you, purify yourselves, and change your garments." (Genesis 35:2)

"If you forsake the Lord and serve foreign gods, then He will turn and do you harm and consume you, after He has done you good." (Joshua 24:20)

"And they forsook the Lord God of their fathers, who had brought them out of the land of Egypt; and they followed other gods from among the gods of the people who were all around them, and they bowed down to them; and they provoked the Lord to anger. They forsook the Lord and served Baal and the Ashtoreths." (Judges 2:12-13)

"Yet they would not listen to their judges, but they played the harlot with other gods, and bowed down to them. They turned quickly from the way in which their fathers walked, in obeying the commandments of the Lord; they did not do so." (Judges 2:17)

Gods without creating power

"They have also built the high places of Baal, to burn their sons with fire for burnt offerings to Baal, which I did not command or speak, nor did it come into my mind." (Jeremiah 19:5)

"Are there any among the idols of the nations that can cause rain? Or can the heavens give showers? Are You not He, O Lord our God? Therefore we will wait for You, since You have made all these." (Jeremiah 14:22)

God's that neither see nor hear

"Their idols are silver and gold, the work of men's hands. They have mouths, but they do not speak: eyes they have, but they do not see; they have ears, but they do not hear; noses they have, but they do not smell; they have hands, but they do not handle; feet they have, but they do not walk; Nor do they mutter through their throat. Those who make them are like them: so is everyone who trusts in them." (Psalm 115:4-8)

Empty things

"And do not turn aside; for then you would go after empty things which cannot profit or deliver, for they are nothing." (1 Samuel 12:21)

What is idolatry of?

Worshipping images
"You shall not make for yourself a carved image - any likeness of anything that is in heaven above, or that is in the earth beneath, or that is in the water under the earth." (Exodus 20:4)

Idol worship
"But if your heart turns away so that you do not hear, and are drawn away, and worship other gods and serve them, I announce to you today that you shall surely perish; you shall not prolong your days in the land which you cross over the Jordan to go in and possess." (Deuteronomy 30:17-18)

"I am the Lord your God, who brought you out of the land of Egypt; open your mouth wide, and I will fill it." (Psalm 81:10)

Worship of creatures
"And take heed, lest you lift your eyes to heaven, and when you see the sun, the moon, and the stars, all the host of heaven, you feel driven to worship them and serve them, which the Lord your God has given to all the peoples under the whole heaven as a heritage." (Deuteronomy 4:19)

"They shall spread them before the sun and the moon and all the host of heaven, which they have loved and which they have served and after which they have walked, which they have sought and which they have worshiped. They shall not be gathered nor buried; they shall be like refuse on the face of the earth." (Jeremiah 8:2)

Worship of angels

"Let no one cheat you of your reward, taking delight in false humility and worship of angels, intruding into those things which he has not seen, vainly puffed up by his fleshly mind, and not holding fast to the Head, from whom all the body, nourished and knit together by joints and ligaments, grows with the increase that is from God." (Colossians 2:18-19)

"Now I, John, saw and heard these things. And when I heard and saw, I fell down to worship before the feet of the angel who showed me these things. Then he said to me, see that you do not do that. For I am your fellow servant, and of your brethren the prophets, and of those who keep the words of this book. Worship God." (Revelation 22:8-9)

Sacrifices to idols

"And shed innocent blood, the blood of their sons and daughters, whom they sacrificed to the idols of Canaan; and the land was polluted with blood." (Psalm 106:38)

Following idols bid

"Then it shall be, if you by any means forget the Lord your God, and follow other gods, and serve them and worship them, I testify against you this day that you shall surely perish." (Deuteronomy 8:19)

"How shall I pardon you for this? Your children have forsaken Me and sworn by those that are not gods when I had fed them to the full, then they committed adultery and assembled themselves by troops in the harlot's houses." (Jeremiah 5:7)

Give idols place in their heart

"Son of man, these men have set up their idols in their hearts, and put before them that which causes them to stumble into iniquity. Should I let Myself be inquired of at all by them? Therefore speak to them, and say to them, thus says the Lord God: Every one of the house of Israel who sets up his idols in his heart, and puts before him what causes him to stumble into iniquity, and then comes to the prophet, I the Lord will answer him who comes, according to the multitude of his idols."
(Ezekiel 14:3-4)

Prohibition of idolatry

"You shall have no other gods before Me. You shall not make for yourself a carved image - any likeness of anything that is in heaven above, or that is in the earth beneath, or that is in the water under the earth; you shall not bow down to them nor serve them. For I, the Lord your God, am a jealous God, visiting the iniquity of the fathers upon the children to the third and fourth generations of those who hate Me." (Exodus 20:3-5)

"And do not become idolaters as were some of them. As it is written, The people sat down to eat and drink, and rose up to play. Nor let us commit sexual immorality, as some of them did, and in one day twenty-three thousand fell; nor let us tempt Christ, as some of them also tempted, and were destroyed by serpents; nor complain, as some of them also complained, and were destroyed by the destroyer. Now all these things happened to them as examples, and they were written for our admonition, upon whom the ends of the ages have come. Therefore let him who thinks he stands take heed lest he falls. No temptation has overtaken you except such as is common to man; but God is faithful, who will not allow you to be tempted beyond what you are able, but with the temptation will also make the way of escape, that you may be able to bear it." (1 Corinthians 10:7-13)

Because it is a carnal act
"Now the works of the flesh are evident, which are; adultery, fornication, uncleanness, lewdness, idolatry, sorcery, hatred, contentions, jealousies, outbursts of wrath, selfish ambitions, dissensions, heresies, envy, murders, drunkenness, revelries, and the like; of which I tell you beforehand, just as I also told you in time past, **that those who practice such things will not inherit the kingdom of God**." (Galatians 5:19-21)

Because it is incompatible with serving God
"Now therefore, he said, put away the foreign gods which are among you, and incline your heart to the Lord God of Israel." (Joshua 24:23)

Exhortations against idolatry
"Therefore say to the house of Israel, thus says the Lord God: Repent, turn away from your idols, and turn your faces away from all your abominations. For anyone of the house of Israel, or of the strangers who dwell in Israel, who separates himself from Me and sets up his idols in his heart and puts before him what causes him to stumble into iniquity, then comes to a prophet to inquire of him concerning Me, I the Lord will answer him by Myself. I will set My face against that man and make him a sign and a proverb, and I will cut him off from the midst of My people. Then you shall know that I am the Lord." (Ezekiel 14:6-8)

"And what accord has Christ with Belial? Or what part has a believer with an unbeliever? And what agreement has the temple of God with idols? For you are the temple of the living God. As God has said: I will dwell in them and walk among them. I will be their God, and they shall be My people. Therefore come out from among them and be separated, says the Lord. Do not touch what is unclean, and I will receive you. I will be a Father to you, and you shall be My sons and daughters, says the Lord Almighty." (2 Corinthians 6:15-18)

Forbid it in his house
"You shall burn the carved images of their gods with fire; you shall not covet the silver or gold that is on them, nor take it for yourselves, lest you be snared by it; for it is an abomination to the Lord your God. Nor shall you bring an abomination into your house, lest you be doomed to destruction like it. You shall utterly detest it and utterly abhor it, for it is an accursed thing." (Deuteronomy 7:25-26)

Do not associate with an idolater
"But now I have written to you not to keep company with any- one named a brother, who is sexually immoral, or covetous, or an idolater, or a reviler, or a drunkard, or an extortioner - not even to eat with such a person." (1 Corinthians 5:11)

Witness against
"And saying, men, why are you doing these things? We also are men with the same nature as you, and preach to you that you should turn from these useless things to the living God, who

made the heaven, the earth, the sea, and all things that are in them." (Acts 14:15)

"Moreover you see and hear that not only at Ephesus, but throughout almost all Asia, this Paul has persuaded and turned away many people, saying that sin must die, or you will perish by it. Depend on it, that sin which you would save from the slaughter will slaughter you." (Acts 19:26)

One should not let themselves idolize
"As Peter was coming in, Cornelius met him and fell down at his feet and worshiped him. But Peter lifted him up saying, stand up; I myself am also a man." (Acts 10:25-26)

"Now when the people saw what Paul had done, they raised their voices, saying in the Lycaonian language, the gods have come down to us in the likeness of men! And Barnabas they called Zeus, and Paul, Hermes, because he was the chief speaker. Then the priest of Zeus, whose temple was in front of their city, brought oxen and garlands to the gates, intending to sacrifice with the multitudes. But when the apostles Barnabas and Paul heard this, they tore their clothes and ran in among the multitude, crying out and saying, men, why are you doing these things? We also are men with the same nature as you, and preach to you that you should turn from these useless things to the living God, who made the heaven, the earth, the sea, and all things that are in them." (Acts 14:11-15)

148

Idolaters forget God

"Then it shall be, if you by any means forget the Lord your God, and follow other gods, and serve them and worship them, I testify against you this day that you shall surely perish."
(Deuteronomy 8:19)

Awakens the wrath of God

"But you shall destroy their altars, break their sacred pillars, and cut down their wooden images for you shall worship no other god, for the Lord, whose name is Jealous, is a jealous God."
(Exodus 34:13-14)

"They said, repent now everyone of his evil way and his evil doings, and dwell in the land that the Lord has given to you and your fathers forever and ever. Do not go after other gods to serve them and worship them, and do not provoke Me to anger with the works of your hands, and I will not harm you. Yet you have not listened to Me, says the Lord, that you might provoke Me to anger with the works of your hands to your own hurt."
(Jeremiah 25:5-7)

It is shameful in the eyes of God

"For we have spent enough of our past lifetime in doing the will of the Gentiles - when we walked in lewdness, lusts, drunkenness, revelries, drinking parties, and abominable idolatries."
(1 Peter 4:3)

Breaks the covenant of God

"When I have brought them to the land flowing with milk and honey, of which I swore to their fathers, and they have eaten and filled themselves and grown fat, then they will turn to other gods and serve them; and they will provoke Me and break My covenant." (Deuteronomy 31:20)

Terrible in the eyes of the Lord;

What the Gentiles sacrifice, they sacrifice to demons and not to God. (1 Corinthians 10:20)

"But to those who are self-seeking and do not obey the truth, but obey unrighteousness - indignation and wrath." (Romans 2:8)

"But outside are dogs and sorcerers and sexually immoral and murderers and idolaters and murderers, and whoever loves and practices a lie. (Revelation 22:15)

"Do you not know that the unrighteous will not inherit the kingdom of God? Do not be deceived. Neither fornicators, nor idolaters, nor adulterers, nor homosexuals, nor sodomites, nor thieves, nor covetous, nor drunkards, nor revilers, nor extortioners will inherit the kingdom of God." (1 Corinthians 6:9-10)

An idolater who does not repent to Jesus, and become born again, there is <u>no</u> salvation for
"But the cowardly, unbelieving, abominable, murderers, sexually immoral, sorcerers, **idolaters**, and all liars shall have their part in the lake which burns with fire and brimstone, which is the second death." (Revelation 21:8)

It is written

"Jesus Christ is the same yesterday, today, and forever."
(Hebrews 13:8)

Notes;

_____

_____

_____

_____

_____

_____

_____

_____

_____

_____

CHAPTER 14

Truth and lies

The truth

The Bible is consists of 66 books. Thirty-nine in the Old Testament and 27 in the New Testament.

Lie

Anything that goes against God's word is a lie.

Truth

"All Scripture is given by inspiration of God, and is profitable for doctrine, for reproof, for correction, for instruction in righteousness, that the man of God may be complete, thoroughly equipped for every good work." (2 Timothy 3:16-17)

"For God so loved the world that He gave His only begotten Son, that whoever believes in Him should not perish but have everlasting life." (John 3:16)

God cannot lie

Can and will God go against his own words? No. God cannot and will never lie. It is not in His nature.

"God is not a man, that He should lie, nor a son of man, that He should repent. Has He said, and will He not do? Or has He spoken, and will He not make it good?" (Numbers 23:19)

-God cannot lie. (Titus 1:2)

"The grass withers, the flower fades, but the word of our God stands forever." (Isaiah 40:8)

"Heaven and earth will pass away, but My words will by no means pass away." (Luke 21:33)

It is solely that God will or can lie. (Hebrews 6:18)

The lie and the spirit of delusion
This spirit will only come with lies and deception into your life. Delusion will come in such a subtle way that you simply believe what comes to you through your thought life.

When you read the Bible, the devil will try itself in many ways. The first thing that happens is that he will do everything he can, stopping you from reading the Bible. When you sit down with the Word of God, the thoughts start to flow like an Indy car race. Here it is essential to discipline yourself by reading and ponder the word every day.

The Bible says
"For the weapons of our warfare are not carnal but mighty in God for pulling down strongholds, casting down arguments and every high thing that exalts itself against the knowledge of God,

bringing every thought into captivity to the obedience of
Christ." (2 Corinthians 10:4-5)

"We are of God. He who knows God hears us: he who is not of
God does not hear us. By this we know the spirit of truth and the
spirit of error." (1 John 4:6)

This spirit has only one main goal; That you shall not start to do
or understand the Lord's commandments and that you should
not get any revelations in the Word. It works hard through the
churches and your thought life. They take you far into the plains
so that you cannot grasp the truth of God's word.

When you are attacked from all angles, you must bind every
thought that is not from God. (2 Corinthians 10:5)
This is a discernment of spirits and everyone must train in this
matter. You've lived with your thought life from birth; Now is
the time to expose Satan how he works through your thought
life.

Go into your room as it is written in Matthew 6:6, and the essential sanctification in Ephesians 6:1-9. These two things must be
on your daily agenda. Your thought life must be revealed, and
the Holy Spirit will show you when you get started.

The sword of the Spirit is the word of God. (Ephesians 6:17)
You must be rooted in the word, then to sort out your thoughts
becomes easier. Easier to distinguish between lies and truths.
Satan is going to shoot fiery darts at you from all angles. Your

154

faith in God's written Word, like the Bible, says you should ponder and meditate on every single day.
-This will be your shield so you can expose and resist the attacks.

In therapy to get rid of God
One of the major newspapers in Norway wrote in the autumn of 2014, one story about a former Norwegian minister, who had a turbulent life and was now in therapy to **forget God**.

The Bible shows us in all simplicity what must be done.
"Jesus answered and said to him; most assuredly, I say to you, unless one is born again, he cannot see the kingdom of God." (John 3:3)

This newspaper wrote;
We are a group that meets each other regularly, and we all are in therapy to get rid of God.

What was happening here? A minister who is in therapy to forget God?
-This sounded dramatic. But what happened? He has never been born again, never repented 100%, never turned away from his sinful life.

At some point in his life, he found himself into the religious state church in Norway, and anyone who has a vivid life with the Lord and His written word knows that a lying spirit is the central pillar of this type of "churches."

This priest does not distinguish between Satan and God's voice at all and then takes it mostly for good fish.

If you let Satan get a stronghold in your thoughts, you will be caught.
-Jesus shows us how to handle this in Matthew 4.

We see that Jesus in Matthew 4:4, 6, 10, how Jesus only used the written Word of God when Satan tempted him.

We read further in Matthew 4:6, here we see that Satan is quoting Psalm 91:11-12: If you are the Son of God, throw yourself down. For it is written; He shall give his angels charge over you, and in their hands, they shall bear you up, lest you dash your foot against a stone.

Look what is written in Psalm 91:11-12.
V11. "For He shall give His angels charge over you, to keep you in all your ways." V12. "In their hands they shall bear you up, lest you dash your foot against a stone."

In Matthew 4:6, Satan quotes the scripture wrong. Elegantly he does not say anything about the last line in verse 11.
-To keep you in all your ways.

Satan sends his fiery mendacious darts constantly. Your responsibility is to stay close to the Lord and His written word. You must continuously grow in discernment to be able to understand.

156

"You are of your father the devil, and the desires of your father you want to do. He was a murderer from the beginning, and does not stand in the truth, because there is **no** truth in him. When he speaks a lie, he speaks from his own resources, for he is a liar and the father of it." (John 8:44)

"My sheep hear My voice, and I know them, and they follow Me. And I give them eternal life, and they shall never perish; neither shall anyone snatch them out of My hand."
(John 10:27-28)

Our faith in the written Word of God overcome this world.
(1 John 5:4)

When Jesus walked on this earth, He was 100% man and 100% God. He had no advantages over us that live on earth today. Jesus had to fight against Satan the same way as we have today. Jesus used the written word of God - that He would come out as the triumphing Lord that He is.

Jesus came to do the Father's will and gave us the keys to how we should implement what is the Father's will for us today.

It is only the power of the revealed word which will make you a winner over this world, where Satan and millions of demons exist. The power is available when you believe and act on God's written Word.

Satan and the demons are here only to destroy everything you do. (John 10:10)

-Everything that you will do for the Lord and others. So what do you do with this? Make sure you are rooted in the word of God, spend time in your room (Matthew 6:6) and live in the daily breakdown of yourself. (The flesh)
When you, together with this start to preach the GospelGospel, you learn quickly to apply the word of God in the same way that Jesus did in Matthew 4.

Let's take a look at an example of a delusion that got a stronghold through someone that accepted a wrong thought.

The following, I have heard countless times
He or she works as a self-employed, or are employed in a company. The person is working six days a week and has a physically hard job. When he comes home from work, it is normal that this person is tired and exhausted. Besides, family and home also require time.

I preach that all Christians shall go out in the world and preach the GospelGospel, and this person also must do this. Then it comes; It is written: six days shalt thou labor, and I do that. Then I have no more time and power to preach the GospelGospel, and not everybody shall preach the GospelGospel either! Otherwise, it had not been written; Six days you shall labor.

But does it say that you shall work like everyone else in this world six days of the week? If not, what kind of job are you going to do in those six days?

Let's see what the scripture says

Six days shalt thou labor. Working in Hebrew is: mla'kah, it means; Ministry. If you then work six days, you shall do your ministry in the same way.

Truth

"For I am not ashamed of the gospel of Christ, for it is the power of God to salvation, for everyone who believes, for the Jew first and also for the Greek." (Romans 1:16)

We must go forward in the power of the Spirit, with the Spirit's gift in our lives, and stand victoriously after having done everything in our Lord Jesus' Name. (Ephesians 6:13)

By this, we know that we love God's children

"By this, we know that we love the children of God, when we love God and keep His commandments." (1 John 5:2)

Love of God

What is love for God? And what kind of love is it that Jehovah the Father accept? For this is the love of God, **when we keep His commandments**. (1 John 5:2-3)

"He who does not love does not know God, for God is love." (1 John 4:8)

"And you shall love the Lord your God with all your heart, with all your soul, with all your mind, and with all your strength. This is the first commandment." (Mark 12:30)

Backbiting

Backbiting is something that most people like non-believers as believers. That it floats poison out of our mouths, about some-one which, of course, is not present.

-To listen to slander is the same as participating in it.

The Bible says

"For rebellion is as the sin of witchcraft, and stubbornness is as iniquity and idolatry. Because you have rejected the word of the Lord, He also has rejected you from being king."

(1 Samuel 15:23)

Backbiting is rebellion against God. To slander, the Bible de-scribes as to try to take someone's life.

"For by your words you will be justified, and by your words you will be condemned." (Matthew 12:37)

Warnings against backbiting

The Bible is obvious in this field. Backbiting is something that is prohibited for all Christians. Any backbiting is a sin.

Backbiting is like candy. We say we do not like it, but when it's within our reach, we cannot resist it. We suddenly get an ap-petite for knowing what we do not know about others, negative or positive.

Why is it so hard to quit?
Proverbs 18:8 says; "The words of a talebearer are like tasty tri-fles, and they go down into the inmost body."

160

"Do not speak evil of one another, brethren. He who speaks evil of a brother and judges his brother, speaks evil of the law and judges the law. But if you judge the law, you are not a doer of the law but a judge." (James 4:11)

"Therefore, laying aside all malice, all deceit, hypocrisy, envy, and all **evil speaking**." (1 Peter 2:1)

"Whoever secretly slanders his neighbor, him I will destroy; The one who has a haughty look and a proud heart, him I will not endure." (Psalm 101:5)

God's wrath over injustice
"For the wrath of God is revealed from heaven against all ungodliness and unrighteousness of men, who suppress the truth in unrighteousness." (Romans 1:18)

"But those things which proceed out of the mouth come from the heart, and they defile a man." (Matthew 15:18)

"For out of the heart proceed evil thoughts, murders, adulteries, fornications, thefts, false witness, blasphemies." (Blasphemy also means evil speaking) (Matthew 15:19)

Notes;

_____

_____

CHAPTER 15

Fear God and keep His commandments

For a long time, it has been proclaimed; Jesus loves you, and He has a wonderful plan for your life. Jesus is only love etc.

But do we find coverage for this in the Bible, that we should just preach a God who loves us? No, we don't.

But what we find is a God who loves us unimaginably high, but in the same Bible, we read that He is a God of wrath that we must fear.

The Bible says in Ecclesiastes 12:13 - Fear God and keep His commandments, for this is man's all.

The flood
The Lord regretted that He had made man on the earth.
(Genesis 6:6)
Of all that God had created, He found only one righteous.
(Genesis 7:1)

Then He rescued the one righteous and his family from His **wrath** against sin. The flood came, and the Lord destroyed **all** life on earth. Only Noah and those who were with him in the ark survived. (Genesis 7:23)

Sodom and Gomorrah

"Then the Lord rained brimstone and fire on Sodom and Gomorrah, from the Lord out of the heavens. So He overthrew those cities, all the plain, all the inhabitants of the cities, and what grew on the ground." (Genesis 19:24-25)

185000 slaughtered by an angel

"Then the angel of the Lord went out, and killed in the camp of the Assyrians one hundred and eighty-five thousand; and when people arose early in the morning, there were the corpses all dead." (Isaiah 37:36)

"Jesus Christ is the same yesterday, today, and forever." (Hebrews 13:8)

Fear God and give him glory! (Revelation 14:6-7)

"So on a set day Herod, arrayed in royal apparel, sat on his throne and gave an oration to them. And the people kept shouting, the voice of a god and not of a man! Then immediately an angel of the Lord struck him, because he did not give glory to God. And he was eaten by worms and died." (Acts 12:21-23)

Yahweh

He is the self-existent God. Yahweh is the Father himself. When we pray, we **shall** give thanks to Him. It is He who is the boss and who gave all the authority to His only begotten Son, Jesus Christ.

"And whatever you do in word or deed, do all in the name of the Lord Jesus, giving thanks to God the Father through Him." (Colossians 3:17)

He is a jealous God. (Exodus 20:5)
He is the God of wrath. (Jeremiah 44:8)

He is the God who allowed his Son to be whipped and crucified because of unimaginably great love for us humans. (John 3:16)

He is not only the Creator, cause He never stopped to create.
He is; Elohim - our eternal Creator. (Genesis 1:1)

Yahweh is;
El-Olam; Eternal God. (Genesis 21:33)
El-Shaddai; Our Sustainer - Almighty God. (Genesis 17:1)
Jehovah Elohim; Jehovah God. (Genesis 2:4)
Elohim Macheslanu; God our rescue. (Psalm 62:8)
Rohi; The Lord, our Shepherd. (Psalm 23:1)
Jehovah El Nas; The Forgiving God. (Psalm 99:8)
Jehovah El-Emunah; The faithful God. (Deuteronomy 7:9)
Jehovah El Magowr; The source of living water. (Jeremiah 2:13)
Alpha & Omega; The Beginning and the end.
(Revelation 21:6)

Fear of God
"The fear of the Lord is the beginning of knowledge, but fools despise wisdom and instruction." (Proverbs 1:7)

"And He said to them, take heed and beware of **covetousness,** for one's life does not consist in the abundance of the things he possesses." (Luke 12:15)

Covetousness; Greek: pleonexia. It means; Greed.

"It is a fearful thing to fall into the hands of the living God." (Hebrews 10:31)

"And do not fear those who kill the body but cannot kill the soul. But rather fear Him who is able to destroy both soul and body in hell." (Matthew 10:28)

"And His mercy is on those who fear Him from generation to generation." (Luke 1:50)

The Bible says in Luke 15:1; **All** the tax collectors and the sinners drew near to Him to hear Him.
Here, we can see that all tax collectors and sinners drew themselves near to Jesus. They were attracted to Him because the truth was preached, and the light in Him has shown.
-Now you go and do the same.

When the truth is preached, the sinners will come.
It is not hard to understand why so little things are happening in today's church. It is **Jesus** who must be the centerpiece of any thinking and action. It is not the miracles we shall seek, but He who is the creator of the miracles. When we receive His heart towards the lost and defeated, when you obey His commandments, then signs and wonders follow.

-For **His glory,** not our own.

The Pharisees and the scribes murmured because Jesus ate and stayed with sinners. (Luke 15:2)

Today's congregation murmur and doubt what is being done on the street is true and necessary.
-They're Christians, within its four walls.

We must have our eyes on Jesus
Miracles are commonplace, and all sorts of sinners you will encounter. Envy and internal conflicts, we must lay aside and stick to what the Lord says; Do everything in love.

In the Philippines, I experienced Luke 15:2 constantly. It was a constant battle.

The Lord, our God, is not impressed by the church's attitude and actions when He says; The harvest truly is plentiful, but the workers are few. (Matthew 9:37)

We have a huge responsibility to pray to the Lord to send forth laborers into His harvest! (Matthew 9:38)

Street work
On the streets of the Philippines, I preached to gays, transsexuals, prostitute, drug dealers, gang members, liars, and all kinds of different sinners. God was with me, and the people were healed in droves. Creative miracles happened several times, and people got new body parts.

When we make ourselves available, the Lord will use you.
When you take the Lord seriously, He will take you seriously.

I'll never forget it

One day while I am eating breakfast in the house, something happened in the backyard. The door was open so that I could see out, and there stood a very feminine man dressed as a woman. 'What is this' I thought and went out.

-Hello, I said, what can I do for you?
This woman/man got a serious problem to find an answer, and the next seconds felt like minutes.
-I had to ask again.
He looked embarrassed to the ground and answered, «I do not know why I'm here at all.»
-Do you know anyone here? I asked
"No, and I do not know why I am here, I just felt led to go here." He answered.
-It's okay; I know why you're here, I responded and began preaching about Jesus Christ.

This person had been in a motorcycle accident a few days in advance and had terrible pain in the left hip. I shared 1 Peter 2:24, by His stripes you were healed. Then I asked if it was okay that I laid my hand on his hip.
"Yes," he replied.
-So I did and thanked Jesus for by His wounds we are healed. Instantly, he was healed.

When the Lord shows up in this way, it cannot be described in words. He is Yahweh; The self-existent God that manifests Himself through healing. (Exodus 6:3, 15:26)

-I continued to preach the gospel.

His face was now completely changed. Suddenly he started to pull off his clothes (not all) and tried to remove all the makeup with his fingers.

-He constantly apologized for his sins.

All of these had happened because I preached what the Bible says about the kind of sin that this person had in her life and that Jesus died for him so he could have life.

The Holy Spirit is the Spirit of Revelation. (John 14:26)

"For God did not send His Son into the world to condemn the world, but that the world through Him might be saved." (John 3:17)

His sin was revealed.

He started to share little about the contents of the sinful life he had. The contempt towards his actions became more transparent. Suddenly, he understood what kind of worthless and sinful life he lived and that this is not the Lord's will.

-His tears flowed like a waterfall.

It was time for repentance to the Lord.

All heaven rejoices when a sinner repents. (Luke 15:7, 10)

I offered a meal inside the house, which he gladly accepted.

We are all called to preach the gospel of the crucified Christ to sinners to repentance.

They are waiting for you.

Sick and defeated

When you are in areas where the need is tremendous and poverty reigns. People are sick, and to go to a doctor, most of them cannot afford it. If they can go to a doctor, they go out again with a long list of medications that must be purchased. A shopping list in one hand and an empty food cup in the other.

Love is a lost chapter in their lives. But in their darkness, you have arrived. You are laying your hands full of the Lord's love on the shoulder of this person. He recognized something when he sees your shining face full of the Holy Spirit. You start to tell about Jesus, who gave His life on Calvary because He loves you so much. Now, the first cornerstone is laid. (Matthew 21:42)

"Let your light so shine before men, that they may see your good works and glorify your Father in heaven." (Matthew 5:16)

That dear reader, it is the greatest miracle you will experience;
To be the love of Jesus among the least.
The Lord is near to those who have a broken heart.
(Psalm 34:18)

"Receive one who is weak in the faith, but not to disputes over doubtful things." (Romans 14:1)

Testimonies

In my Ministry, I have witnessed countless wonderful miracles.
-Numerous times have other "Christians" done what they can to
trample it down in the mud. There's only one thing to say about
the matter; They are nothing but Satan's workers.

If you are functioning in discerning between spirits, and you
speak out anything that is not in Scripture, then the Holy Spirit
will show you what you do. If you are not willing to learn from
the Holy Spirit here, you will make your neck stiff, and further
growth and understanding in the Lord are not possible without
repentance.
-Here it is necessary to live a **surrendered** life to the Lord.

This is the same as we read in Luke 15:2.
They think that all of the defeated and the sinners shall come to
them into the church, not they who shall go to them.

The defeated, the poor, the orphans, the lost, they have no faith.
-We must go to them.

Therefore the Bible says in the Great Commission; Go.

The lost
We read in Luke 15 from verses 4-6 about the one sheep which
was lost **but was found.**
And from verses 8-9 about one piece of silver that was lost, **but
was found**.
The prodigal son in verses 11-32, the son who left his father and
became lost, was dead and **was found.**

It's all about the Father and His love for the lost in these verses in Luke 15. He wants everyone to come to Him. Yahweh, God, the Father says in the Bible; The whole Heaven rejoices when someone who has gone astray and come back to Him.

What a mighty God we have.

Are you keeping His commandments?
"Preach the word! Be ready in season and out of season. Convince, rebuke, exhort, with all long-suffering and teaching." (2 Timothy 4:2)

Go and preach the gospel. (Matthew 28:18-20)
Love your neighbor as yourself. (Matthew 22:39)

Does it help to have faith if it does not have works?
(James 2:18)

"For the wages of sin is death, but the gift of God is eternal life in Christ Jesus our Lord." (Romans 6:23)

"If you love Me, keep My commandments." (John 14:15)

Notes;

_____

_____

_____

CHAPTER 16

The law of Jante

They call it the Law of Jante. Nobody likes it. However, most people in Northern Europe practice a large part of it.

The ten rules state that;

1. "You are not to think you're anyone special or that you're better than us."

2. You're not to think you are as good as we are.

3. You're not to think you are smarter than we are.

4. You're not to convince yourself that you are better than we are.

5. You're not to think you know more than we do.

6. You're not to think you are more important than we are.

7. You're not to think you are good at anything.

8. You're not to laugh at us.

9. You're not to think anyone cares about you.

10. You're not to think you can teach us anything.

11. Perhaps, you don't think we know a few things about you?

Spiritual disorder in a society is characterized by the love of mammon and most of the wicked things. It brings this Pharisaic law of Jante into our society.

Man thinks that he does not need 'God.' Their lives are concerned with their own opinions, achievements, and bliss.

Maybe we do not like the law of Jante much, but it is represented all over in Northern Europe. The law of Jante is practiced where it gets a foothold. The law of Jante is a part of our culture and our daily life and is a perverted version of the Lord's Ten Commandments.
-The law of Jante has created a wrong image of what **true humility** is. True humility is not to think a little about yourself: rather, it is to think a little of yourself.

The Bible says in James 4:6: "God resists the proud, but gives grace to the humble." God cannot be clearer in this statement. If you do not humble yourself, He will not accept you. If you do humble yourself, He will open up His doors for you.
-Here your volition needs to begin.

The Law of Jante comes into our lives as we speak it out toward ourselves and to others. When we accept that others speak condescendingly to us, demons are clinging on. Why? Because in this case goes all the 11 "Jante" bids against God's written word in the Bible.

Read all 11 laws of Jante. While doing so, imagine that it is Satan who reads those up for you, and behind him stands an army of demons.
-Then you see it.

God's Ten Commandments.

1st Commandment
"You shall have no other gods before Me." (Exodus 20:3)

2nd Commandment
"You shall not make for yourself a carved image - any likeness of anything that is in heaven above, or that is in the earth beneath, or that is in the water under the earth; you shall not bow down to them nor serve them. For I, the Lord your God, am a jealous God, visiting the iniquity of the fathers upon the children to the third and fourth generations of those who hate Me, but showing mercy to thousands, to those who love Me and keep My commandments." (Exodus 20:4-6)

3rd Commandment
"You shall not take the name of the Lord your God in vain, for the Lord will not hold him guiltless who takes His name in vain." (Exodus 20:7)

4th Commandment

"Remember the Sabbath day, to keep it holy. Six days you shall labor and do all your work, but the seventh day is the Sabbath of the Lord your God. In it you shall do no work; you, nor your son, nor your daughter, nor your male servant, nor your female servant, nor your cattle, nor your stranger who is within your gates. For in six days, the Lord made the heavens and the earth, the sea, and all that is in them, and rested the seventh day. Therefore the Lord blessed the Sabbath day and hallowed it." (Exodus 20:8-11)

5th Commandment

"Honor your father and your mother, that your days may be long upon the land which the Lord your God is giving you." (Exodus 20:12)

6th Commandment

"You shall not murder." (Exodus 20:13)

7th Commandment

"You shall not commit adultery." (Exodus 20:14)

8th Commandment

"You shall not steal." (Exodus 20:15)

9th Commandment

"You shall not bear false witness against your neighbor." (Exodus 20:16)

10th Commandment

"You shall not covet your neighbor's house; you shall not covet your neighbor's wife, nor his male servant, nor his female servant, nor his ox, nor his donkey, nor anything that is your neighbor's." (Exodus 20:17)

The law of Jante

Perhaps, it is only an author's imagination written down on a sheet of paper, which was later to find on top of many tables. But when you declare with your mouth or go in agreement with the thoughts that go against God's written word the Bible, then you have opened the door to the dark spiritual army.

You have allowed them to annoy you - not as you want, but as they will; Or as it is done here with a pen from the author's side. As later, when published was read by many. The devil is cunning, and he will use all the tricks that he has learned over the past thousands of years, to sneak sin into your life. You accept it when you are not born again or rooted in God's word, or you hang around with people who are full of disbelief. (2 Corinthians 6:14)

The years passed by, and you live a religious lifestyle. Then you will die of natural causes and will fall short of salvation. -The disaster indeed became a fact.

We must always make sure that we live in God's written word. In today's modern society, this is an essential thing that you must do, from getting up in the morning to going back to bed.

Namely, to fill you with Jesus in prayer and through the scriptures.

Are you one who speaks out or think the law of Jante toward others and yourself, then there is only one thing to do - that is to get down on your knees and speak out the most powerful a man can do; 'God, forgive me for I have sinned.'
Then be specific with the Lord about the matter, then He will forgive you.

The Bible says
"Now the works of the flesh are evident, which are: adultery, fornication, uncleanness, lewdness, idolatry, sorcery, hatred, contentions, jealousies, outbursts of wrath, selfish ambitions, dissensions, heresies, envy, murders, drunkenness, revelries, and the like: of which I tell you beforehand, just as I also told you in time past, that those who practice such things **will not inherit the kingdom of God**." (Galatians 5:19-21)

Those who do such things shall not inherit the kingdom of God. The Lord is obvious in His speech. This type of action or behavior will depart your chances of going to heaven. Here too, it is not difficult to draw a parallel line from the Law of Jante to the works of the flesh.

We shall live in spiritual fruits, not in the flesh. A close unity with Him must characterize your daily journey with the Lord, and sanctification is something we as Christians must continuously work with. (Ephesians 6:1-9)

Jesus has made us a royal priesthood to proclaim His greatness. (1 Peter 2:9-10)

"For you are all sons of God through faith in Christ Jesus." (Galatians 3:26)

Let the Holy Spirit be your teacher, not the spirit of this world, or other infidel believers.

Notes;

_____

_____

_____

_____

_____

_____

_____

_____

178

Notes;

_____

_____

_____

_____

_____

_____

_____

_____

_____

_____

_____

CHAPTER 17

Platform preacher

Facebook; Platform preachers' mecca

The whole world is on Facebook. Suddenly you have 'friends' from places that you never thought of. Very often, I receive friend requests from Pastors in India, Pakistan, Africa, and other countries in that direction of the map.

Suddenly, the messages are starting to show up in your inbox, with a very lovely 'thank you' that you accepted their friend requests. They tell you further that they are praying for you and your ministry every single day. They read through everything you've posted on Facebook and will then quickly form a picture of who you are. Then you are starting to get personalized messages. We see the Lord using you significantly in healing etc. Come to India, **the Lord has called you here**. We will arrange a place and invite all the people in the villages. It never gets less than 10 thousand people at the meeting. We do this only for the glory of the Lord. **You've been chosen.**

Finally, 'I' will be allowed to stand on a 'big' platform. Imagine that someone has seen what I have felt for so long. Is it not to just say, 'Yes I will come,' obtain a ticket, land in India with newly polished shoes, and be escorted directly to the platform?

Wow, I shall be picked up at the airport and brought out to the vast plains where the campaign shall be. It is inevitable, the big platform, which is built for the international preacher who has the 'power' with him.

The evening comes, and the campaign is about to begin. It's time to bring thousands upon thousands to the Lord. From spectator place you hear a man's roar of dimensions! Gazing out over the plains, you see thousands upon thousands who have come to listen to the 'anointed' preacher. The Pastors are on the platform and clap your way to the microphone. All eyes are on you now crossing the stage with your shiny shoes. You grab the mic, and a large 'Haaaaalleeeeeeluuuujaaaaaa' rang out across the plains. The mass respond with a ten times greater Hallelujah. -It's almost like the Crusades of Reinhard Bonnke in Africa.

When these invitations have come, it emerges gradually in conversation that they already have one or more people who are willing to sponsor around 5000 USD for this gospel crusade. They 'need' the only remaining of the budget of 10,000 USD from you.

5000 USD you must up with because you are 'called' to India.

The 5000 USD, which they say is half the campaign price, is the **entire** campaign price. And of 5000 USD, 4000 USD ends up in the pocket of the so-called 'brother,' which pointed out emphatically that you were called to India.

What looks like a great invitation is; People who are only looking for dollars, in arranging the healing campaigns for the 'anointed' preachers.

All of us must be very careful
As ravenous wolves come in sheep's clothing, and by their fruits you shall know them. (Matthew 7:15-16)

The first Crusades we had in the Philippines was a little different
Nothing of the preparatory work I left to others. I was involved in everything. I handpicked workers from a local church, and they were not chosen for their qualifications, but by their willingness to participate in the Lord's work.
-When we go, we always equip other believers.

We decided on an area and began to pray for it.
Many things need to be arranged before a campaign. Posters and flyers should be designed and printed. A whole day goes by handing out leaflets to all households in the area where the campaign should be.

Whatever needed to be done, I was involved in it.
-The shiny shoes were left home in Norway.

When working together like this, you are learning to know each other. It is necessary when all workers have tasks during the campaign.

The campaign day

The message was given sometimes from a truck or a stage. It rang out over the countryside from the massive speakers. After the message was finished, it was time to summon those who were sick.

The following happened;
The team I used were at about 8-10 people. When we should pray for the sick, the team was lined up next to each other with their line of people to pray for.

Most of the time, I was watching it all from the side where I was standing. The team stood available that day, and miracles they all experienced.

One time we had a campaign deep in the bush in the Philippines. There we lend a basketball facility with grandstands on one side and a stage on the other side. What we did right before the start was to take all the children upon the scene. All of them got their chair as they sat quietly as a mouse on. They were the V.I.P for this afternoon. Children are always pushed away. This act is not right: therefore, I did it this way.

It is the people who shall be reached

Our ego with shiny shoes is not what shall shine. It's the name above all names, Jesus Christ, that shall have 100% focus. Jesus Christ, our Almighty Savior, and the fantastic work that He did on Calvary. And the kids, we need to have them with us, not pushing them away.

The power comes from the revelation of the word, not the size of the platform
When you spend time with the Lord as you live in sanctification, in proclaiming the powerful work of Calvary, Jesus dead and risen, to sinners, to repentance, the power is released. More info in 1 Corinthians 2:1-5.

He gave His life - No one could take it.

The Bible says that signs and wonders will follow believers. Who is the one who believes? All those who believe.
-His Name shall be lifted, not ours.

Tourist missionary
There have been invitations from 'brothers" in Norway that were in the planning phase for a trip somewhere in Asia. They planned to visit other ministries that some Norwegians had. Plane tickets, hotel rooms, and food would be paid. It was just to fling himself and mark the calendar the time we would be gone.

Quite naturally, I ask these questions; Are you going out on the streets to pray for the sick and preach the Gospel to the lost? Are you going to hand out food to the poor? Will you have separate campaigns while you're down there? Do you intend to arrange it by yourself? Etc.

The answer that came was shocking
No, we have not planned either campaign, distributing food, or out to pray for the sick. My response was the following; If you are traveling to the other side of the earth and visit other min-

istries, it is indeed lovely. But I believe in to be one that comes with the power to the lost sheep. People starve to death on the streets of the areas that we are in, and we will not hand out food? To lie under others' ministries, or be reflected in it - I have no faith for.

One does not at all need to travel to other ministries to learn how we shall do the work for the Lord. We must rely on the Holy Spirit as He is. He will teach us all things because He is the Spirit of Revelations. (John 14:26)

-If we believe the Lord's mission commandment, then we do the walk and the talk by our self.

'Sorry, but I'm not a tourist missionary, I stay at home. Thank you for the invitation.

-That was the answer!

Jesus has called us all out into the big world. It is we who have made small. To have faith to travel, there is barely someone who has. The Bible says go, we say; I do not have it in my heart, or God has not shown or either told me that. Well, it's already revealed to you in the Bible. Why will not you believe in it? What revelations do you think that God will give you when He has already said that in the Bible?

-First, you need to believe, then act, then it happens.

Here is the revelation what the Bible says about to go; Go into **all** the world and preach the Gospel to every creature!
(Mark 16:15)

Now the revelation has been given you, now you act.

CHAPTER 18

Smiloo

The fundraising

Every year at the same time, it comes during prime television time.

-The yearly fundraising.

You get people knocking on your door with big smiles and buckets with a huge sealing line, only to show you that they are 'serious.'

When the authorities collect aid money, they use live television from many of the municipalities, with celebrities such as TV hosts. It does not take long before millions upon millions are collected.

Do we ever hear anything at all about the details rounded this fundraiser?

-It's not much they share with the donors.

Imagine how exciting it had been to see in prime tv time: where and how this money was used.

But unfortunately, this is where the control prevails.

The newspapers write a few lines; Much of the money that has been collected is placed in a bank account or invested in a fund. -It's not exactly what they said during the fundraiser while the studio was full of celebrities.

Approximately 22,000 children die every day of hunger and poverty.
Millions are being collected, and they are investing in a fund? There is something wrong with this picture.
-They will all be held accountable before the Lord one day.

Give, and it shall be given unto you
For a long time, I had thought about involving myself more in humanitarian work and not just to donate a monthly amount somewhere. I was about to start praying about the matter, but the Lord came me forestalled.
-Thoughts and images began to stream in.

The start-up
The Lord put something on my heart, and it went along with the written Word of the Bible. I approached a friend in the Philippines, and we agreed to start to give food to the needy.

This guy had access to a small pickup, and he filled it with food, and out towards the Rizal park, it went. Now it was all suddenly a reality. Smiloo, the Norwegian humanitarian organization, was now operational.

Many mouths were filled in the first period, and slowly it all started to grow. Many places in this part of the world, do not own the majority of the site where they have a small cardboard shack on. They ask many times not the owner of the lot either, but just sets up a small shed where there is a possibility and betting that it goes well. It is in these squatter areas we did most of the work in the beginning.

The sick

My friend, he had prayed for sick people before. But to actively look for those that he had not done. Then one day, just before the food distribution should start, he got this over the phone; Today, during food distribution, ask the following to all of those who have come. And when you ask them, not just ask it like any questions, but sit down with each one of them and ask the following; If you have any pain or illnesses in your body, tell me now.

-Here, he got a challenge, and he took it. He knew well that it went along with the written word of God, and acted accordingly. People had many different diseases and pains, and many were healed that day.
-On the next food distribution, praying for the sick and frail was commonplace.

Landfilling

While distributing food on the streets began, we also started the food distribution at the local landfill. We did a little surveillance of the area first, and then we started the food distribution to approximately 100-150 children. Most of the children were from 3-8 years old, living in the landfill area.

-It breaks your heart when you see this little one comes walking through the smelling garbage to get food. They bring a small cup and a saucer. Some have shoes, and others have not. Most of the parents worked at the landfill, not as employees, but in search of recyclable materials to sell so they could have to the daily bread.

Approximately 5-10 US Dollars per week they can earn if they work hard.
One thing that we in the Western part of the world do not think a lot about is; The garbage we throw in, e.g., Scandinavia, includes all sorts of waste, both new and old. But in the Philippines, they do not throw anything that is not necessary to throw.

There is not any kind of recycling, and hazardous waste can be found anywhere in these landfills. Many did not have shoes, and the people's clothes barely hang on their bodies. In places like these, all believers in the Western world should go and try to minister so that they could see the distress up close.

Most of these people have some kind of disease in their bodies. Consider what would happen if you came to a similar place with a faith that was according to Mark 16:18. Then you will experience the power of the Lord immediately when you start to act on your beliefs.

Spiritual soup station
One day when I was out and was preaching the gospel, the Lord showed me the following; The people in the Philippines need food. But it is not the solid food they need first and foremost. "It's Me they need first," the Lord said. Great I thought, in the

next food distribution, we will give them the word of God at 1 p.m. and food at 2 p.m. The Lord is simple in His opinions and actions. It is only those who 'believe' that complicate them to such a degree.

Cleft lip

An acquaintance came home after an extended summer vacation on Mindanao in the southern Philippines. He said to me the following when we met; Have a look at this, please. In his telephone, he had a picture of a little girl, who lived near the place where he had spent most of his vacation. The girl was two years old and was born with a cleft palate. When I saw that image, it stuck immediately in my heart. I do not recall that I've seen people before with open lip and palate. In Norway, children that are born with this defect are having surgery before they go home from the hospital. Here in the Philippines, it's different.

They have absolutely no systems that address these types of problems. If the family has money, they can get the child operated, but in most cases, they barely have money for the bus fee home from the hospital.

When I went home from my friend that night, it was with a sad heart. From 11 p.m. that evening, I sat on the computer and remained there until early in the morning the next day. The whole night I prayed and cried.

During the night, the Lord had shown me how it was possible to help children like this. In the Philippines, it is like many other places in Asia; The hospitals are private and very expensive.

-But where costly private hospitals are, the Lord had a solution.

What the Lord has shown to me was a private organization that had specialized in issues like this. I got in touch with them, and they told me that they had an agreement with the best private hospital in the city where we have started our work.

Now it was time to change gear. Flyers were designed in Norway and sent to the Philippines for printing and into stapled up in 8 different municipal houses.

The flyers stated that we were looking for children who were born with a cleft palate. It did not take long before the first SMS ticked in. Some weeks later, the first child was on the way to the hospital for a new life.

When a child grows up with this kind of disability, they become many times a victim of bullying.
-A life of isolation is, most of the time, what awaits.

Shame is something that these kids feel on. Many are dumped on the streets when they are newborn infants or left behind with other family members. It is not only the child who needs help in these situations, but more often, the whole family.

The Gospel of Christ Jesus goes hand in hand with humanitarian work. (Where it is possible)

Few people in this town knew about this possibility in the private hospital. Think about this; Children are born within walking distance to a private hospital. And this hospital has an agreement with an international organization that pays all the expenses for the surgery. Therefore, we hung up posters where we searched for these children.

If you live in a part of the world where the Internet and information about all sorts of things flow, you can quickly become a significant asset in these parts of the world.

Here's an example; A place in the Philippines, there is a private hospital. Everyone who lives in this city knows about this place, but very few can afford to go there. When we find children who need surgery and the conversations with parents start, very few of them believe what we are telling them.
-It's free, and it's in the best hospital on the Island.

These hospitals do not announce these kinds of surgeries; Therefore, those who live there will never know it either.
And this the Lord showed to me in prayers, on the Internet, in Norway.
-You see, if you want to be used by the Lord, He will use you.

Malnourished
It is not only in Africa that the children are malnourished. In the Philippines, many children are looking healthy and are going to school every day. But if you know a little bit about malnutrition, it is quite easy to see which children who need your help.

The hair color of the Asian people is black. If you see children with blonde highlights in their hair, this is one of the signs of malnutrition. A thin body with a big round stomach is also a sign that follows. A child who is malnourished from birth may have developed space in the middle of the head with the size of an egg at five years of age. It happens because the body begins first to prey on the muscles, then it starts to prey on the brain when they do not ingest the nutrients they need. These cases of affected children happen to have great difficulty in developing.

The Lord's will is that all Christians should initiate and give everything of ourselves, just as He gave everything at the Calvary.

Biblical attitudes of believers towards the poor

"The righteous considers the cause of the poor, but the wicked does not understand such knowledge." (Proverbs 29:7)

Here scripture says; The **poor**. The Greek word for poor is: dal, and it means; Weak, needy, and poor.

"But whoever has this world's goods, and sees his brother in need, and shuts up his heart from him, how does the love of God abide in Him?" (1 John 3:17)

"So let each one give as he purposes in his heart, not grudgingly or of necessity; for God loves a cheerful giver." (2 Corinthians 9:7)

"He who has pity on the poor lends to the Lord, and He will pay back what he has given." (Proverbs 19:17)

If it is written in the Bible, it is revealed to you, and you can act on it. Jesus walks with the ones who walk, and signs and wonders will follow. (Mark 16:17-18)

Love your neighbor as yourself
Jesus made a total identification against the poor and declared that everything that is done to the least is done to Him. Isaiah 58:10 should be a fundamental principle in our thoughts and our way of life. In the same way, as in the first centuries of believers.

"Pure and undefiled religion before God and the Father is this; To visit orphans and widows in their trouble, and to keep oneself unspotted from the world." (James 1:27)

The Bible says; Love your neighbor as yourself.
(Matthew 22:39)

A Church in Tagbilaran City
When we had food distribution in the landfill, I had some volunteers from a local church in Tagbilaran City. It was one lady in this church that stood out. There was no doubt that she had a big heart for these children.

She was with us several times, and all evolved in a very positive direction. Eventually, we stopped the work on the landfill because we wanted a more permanent solution. Training the children in the Word of God is something that takes time, and is not so easy when you work at the street level.

I asked this lady if it was necessary with food distribution in a specific area.

The answer I already knew since I had been evangelizing many times in this part of the town.

"Yes, there is a great need here," she said, but we have never had the opportunity to do it. It is not difficult to understand that it is not easy when you see hundreds upon hundreds of children with huge needs, no matter where you look around.

-Money is necessary to set up this kind of work, so I gave her an offer to start feeding work. World's biggest smile and a big yes was the answer. And in the following days, the first details in the plan was laid.

A few months later, more than one thousand meals had been served in her church. The kids got both physical and spiritual food. It had become such a big blessing for the neighboring kids that they showed up hours upfront every Saturday.

The workers are growing in the Lord
Without volunteers, this work has been impossible. To see people grow in the Lord, while stomachs of kids are getting filled is just a great miracle to experience. I advise you strongly to find a place where you can get involved something more than to only submit a monthly amount.

The children are now praying for another, and they get healed
The whole congregation was trained to pray for the sick. Healing occurred every time we were out in public. And from the

start, we learned up the children to pray for each other. Eventually, it became quite natural for them to pray for each other, and miracles among the smallest was now something that happened every time we had food distribution.

Here's how it goes. One day had four children stomach aches, and another sat in a corner with a toothache. Then one of the workers calls together all the kids, and they're told that this one has a stomach ache and the other one has a toothache. Then all the children started to pray for the one with pain. Suddenly, no one was sitting in a corner holding his jaw, nor had any more stomach aches, but they all run happily around in the church. Jesus is never late with His promises, and for the children, this is something they take with them in their lives.
-What a mighty God we have.

The need is always just around the corner
One-day, Luz, who was now head of Smiloo's food distribution in Bohol, was out on an errand at the local market. She came across three children who lived in a wooden box with his father. The children were aging in 7, 9, and 11 years old. They had lived in this wooden box approx. Six months and their mother had none of them seen in a long time.

None of the children had gone to school. To read and write - they did not know how to do it. The oldest at 11 years, she weighed 21 kilograms. That is 46,3 pounds.
-They were all brought home to Luz, and she fired up the saucepans. These children became regular visitors the days we

have food distribution. A not long time after they had beautiful green uniforms for school usage.

Faith and Deeds

"What does it profit, my brethren, if someone says he has faith but does not have works? Can faith save him? If a brother or sister is naked and destitute of daily food, and one of you says to them, depart in peace, be warmed and filled, but you do not give them the things which are needed for the body, what does it profit? Thus also faith by itself, if it does not have works, is dead." (James 2:14-17)

How can you do it accordingly?

If you have a heart for others, travel to a country with a lot of poverty, then you will find thousands of needy ones.

-If you do not have a heart for the poor and lost, I have the following question for you. Are you born again?

Scripture clearly says that we shall reach out our hands. Then there's only one thing to do; Get up off the couch, turn on the computer and get hold of an airline ticket.

And before you go, say the following; Thank you, Jesus, that you are with me.

When you arrive at the destination, have your dinner at the Hilton canceled. Instead, go and buy large dinner pots, fill them with food, and bring them to the part of the city where the need is great.

"He who has a generous eye will be blessed, for he gives of his bread to the poor." (Proverbs 22:9)

An acquaintance was going to Manila with his family
He rented and Taxi, and filled the trunk with food. Off they went into an area that had bridges over rivers. Under the first bridge, it lived approx. 100 families. Do we understand this? One hundred families and that under the first bridge.
Here they lived, and many of them were sick. Then it is just to announce that you are going to distribute some food and that you pray for the sick and those with pain.
-Now you have work for the rest of the day.

Then, my friend, you are the love of Christ among the smallest. And healing always happens. Cause the Lord will always follow up on His written promises.

"He answered and said to them, he who has two tunics, let him give to him who has none; and he who has food, let him do likewise." (Luke 3:11)

The story you just read happened in Manila - Philippines. In this city lives approx: 18 million people and 200,000 street children. The need is gigantic!

You are a giant in the Lord Jesus Christ. **Get going**.

198

Notes;

_____

_____

_____

_____

_____

_____

_____

_____

_____

_____

_____

_____

CHAPTER 19

Thank you very much for reading this book

I hope it has been an inspiration to you, and that you will take the plunge into the power ministry our Lord and Savior Jesus Christ has for you.

It is essential to get into a Biblical understanding of who our God is. Lay down your life, surrender everything to the Lord our God. He said that signs and wonders will follow those who believe.

All the old, all of the carnal desires, everything that goes against the Lord's written Word, must be repented from in your life. All knowledge that you need must come from the Lord. He will give to all who are willing to lay down their lives and obey His commandments.

Take it, seek the Lord with all your heart, with all your strength, with all your mind.
Then you will have it.

Stay updated

There are new books on its way. Stay tuned to our website for new releases.

www.SecretRevelations.com

God bless you.
Rune Larsen

Pain or any sickness, be healed in Jesus name!